LEGEND

THE LIFE OF ROY 'CHOPPER' HARTLE

John Gradwell

Published by John Gradwell
Publishing partner: Paragon Publishing, Rothersthorpe
First published 2013
© John Gradwell 2013

ISBN 978-1-78222-089-3

Book design, layout and production management by Into Print
www.intoprint.net
01604 832149

Printed and bound in UK and USA by Lightning Source

MY THANKS TO:

Jimmy Armfield, Tommy Banks, Brian Birch, Bolton Central Library, The Bolton News, Bolton Wanderers Football Club, Andrew Dean, Bryan Edwards, Jean Edwards, Syd Farrimond, The Football League, Phil Gartside, Freddie Goodwin, Carole Gradwell, Philip Gradwell, Helen Gradwell, Ted Green, Barbara Hartle, Dennis Hartle, Jill Hartle, Roy Hartle, Russell Hartle, Doug Holden, Wayne Howarth, Alexander Jackson (The National Football Museum), Francis Lee, Simon Marland, Mike Summerbee, Gordon Taylor, Kath Teece, Pete Vickers, Jimmy Wagg, Councillor John Walsh.

ABOUT THE AUTHOR:

JOHN GRADWELL has worked as a journalist on a number of North West newspapers and spent twenty years as a news sub-editor with the Manchester Evening News. He is a radio comedy writer and dramatist whose first novel, Funnybone, was published in 2012. Born in Great Lever, John has supported Bolton Wanderers since 1961. He is married with a son and a daughter.

For Carole, Philip and Helen

FOREWORD
by
Phil Gartside, Chairman, Bolton Wanderers Football Club

I'm delighted to have been asked to write the foreword to this biography of my great friend Roy Hartle. To any Bolton Wanderers fan born in the baby boomer generation or before, the name "Chopper" Hartle evokes memories of thundering challenges, last-ditch tackles and whole-hearted commitment on the football pitch from a man who spent his entire career at the club.

I vividly remember the first time I saw Roy play. I was eleven years old and it was a Third Round FA Cup match at Burnden Park against Bath City. From the start, I could not believe how tough this guy was. It looked as if a runaway train wouldn't stop him and I almost, but not quite, felt sorry for the wingers whose duty it was to try to get round Roy and stay in one piece.

But Roy wasn't just a football hard man. He was a leader on the pitch who became an inspirational captain of the club. And, of course, he'll be remembered as a vital part of the team which lifted the FA Cup for Bolton in 1958 – fitting compensation for the disappointment he suffered five years earlier when, in his debut season, he was left out of the Wanderers' Cup Final line-up after playing in every other round. It's also a shame that he never won an international cap although he did have the honour to represent the Football League against the Irish League a few months after winning the Cup.

However, much as I relished and valued the playing exploits of this football legend, it is off the field where I have come to know and value him best. Not long after I joined the Bolton Wanderers board in 1989, Roy teamed up with the club's all-time legend Nat Lofthouse to become a match-day host at Burnden Park. The role continued and expanded greatly when the club moved to the Reebok Stadium in 1997 where Roy became a familiar figure, entertaining visitors and putting them at their ease with a quiet, well-spoken manner which totally belied his old playing image. It was extremely appropriate that in 2004 the Emerson Suite at the Reebok was re-named the Roy Hartle Suite in tribute to this football stalwart. It was also fitting that Roy represented the club at the opening of the new Wembley in 2007 when past winners of the FA Cup were welcomed on to the pitch.

Not long after that, everyone at the club was desperately sad to hear that Roy had suffered a debilitating stroke. However, we're all equally delighted that in the years since he has fought back in the manner anyone who knows him would expect from such a strong and determined character.

Roy and his devoted wife Barbara are welcome faces around the place on match days and, hopefully, will be for many years to come. He has been a splendid ambassador for Bolton Wanderers Football Club.

Phil Gartside, Chairman BWFC, June 2013

INTRODUCTION

Ten weeks before Bobby Moore considerately wiped his dirty hands on his white shorts and collected the World Cup from The Queen, Roy Hartle's career in league football ended abruptly. As England's golden boy brandished the Jules Rimet Trophy in front of ninety-three thousand ecstatic fans at Wembley, the Bolton Wanderers stalwart was still coming to terms with the free transfer he'd been handed by the club he'd served with distinction for fourteen years – the one for which he had made 499 appearances. Worse still, it was becoming clear that no other club appeared to want him either.

On the face of it there's little connection between the two events. While it's true that Roy had been described by more than one commentator as the best right back never to play for England, it would appear fanciful in the extreme to directly link him with the country's greatest sporting moment. But when, on March 16th 1966, Roy ran out to play his final league game against Preston North End at Burnden Park, neither he nor most of the 13,961 people present at that Division Two match can have had much of an idea that an era in English football was rapidly coming to an end and that events at Wembley on July 31st that year would deal it a mortal blow.

Now it's a fact that pinpointing decisive historical turning points can be a tricky business. It could be argued that football entered the modern era in 1961 when the players' maximum wage was abolished. Or maybe two years later when George Best, surely the supreme example of the English game's first modern superstar, made his debut for Manchester United. Or it could be located well after England's World Cup triumph, maybe with the introduction of extended TV coverage accompanied by punditry in the 1970s or moves towards greater ground safety in the 1980s and 1990s.

But, for argument's sake let's put the time that football's old era ended and the new one began at the point when the twentieth century was exactly two thirds over. After all, though the upper ceiling of footballers' pay had not been pegged at £20 a week for five years, Roy Hartle still needed to supplement his wages with summer jobs as he had throughout his career as a top-flight footballer. In fact Roy only began to make a really decent salary when he started work as a representative for a wine company in late 1966.

And nineteen-year-old Best only became "El Beatle" on the front pages seven days before Roy's final game, following a dazzling display in United's 5-1 thrashing of Benfica in Lisbon.

This division between the old and the new can be neatly illustrated in the matter of on-field discipline. For twenty-three years after 1937 no Bolton player was sent off until John Higgins got his marching orders for appearing to manhandle the referee during an away match against Sheffield Wednesday in February 1960. And despite being, let's say, one of the more robust practitioners of the full-back's art, Roy Hartle was booked just once throughout his entire career. Although this can be partly explained by his respectful attitude to referees it also demonstrates the more easy-going nature of officials in those days. Contrast that with the change that took place in the decade after Roy retired. His long-time full-back partner Syd Farrimond ended his professional career in 1974, just eight years after Roy, but was sent off three times and received seventeen bookings. In a classic piece of understatement, Syd reckoned: "I didn't think I was any worse than Roy."

Whatever the cut-off point chosen, there is no doubt that Roy played his football in another age entirely. If they didn't exactly kick a tin can around and use jumpers for goalposts, things were very unlike how they are now. It all took place in a Britain that looked, smelled and tasted totally different – one in which I was growing up as a dedicated young Wanderers fan.

There is another link between the Boys of '66 and the tough Bolton legend known to his many fans as "Chopper". For years after England's Wembley victory, that team was nothing more than a little bit special to the public simply because nobody thought that 1966 would be the last time as well as the first that we'd win a World Cup. But as two 1970s tournaments passed without England's participation and the succession of near-misses, blunders and moments of low farce every four years mounted up, we belatedly woke up to the realisation that the only people who'd managed to do this rather special thing needed to be honoured and cherished. That's why the scorer of England's World Cup Final hat-trick, a man lost to football for twenty years, is now Sir Geoff Hurst and one of our foremost sporting ambassadors. People with no first-hand memory of that warm late July afternoon in 1966 now clamour to be photographed with him.

A similar thing, albeit on a less lofty scale, has happened to Roy Hartle. For years after his retirement Roy became a relative stranger to football. When he finished scouting duties in the early Seventies it was another two decades before an even more substantial Bolton legend, Nat Lofthouse, brought him back to the sport as a Wanderers match day host and all-round popular club stalwart. The Roy Hartle Suite at Bolton's Reebok Stadium is eloquent testimony to the regard in which he is now held.

As Roy's wife Barbara proudly declared: "So many people come up to him on match days to shake his hand. He's never been so popular."

In a similar manner to Geoff Hurst and the other boys of '66, the reason for Roy's current popularity is not difficult to understand. As well as being a familiar and reassuring figure, Roy is a member of the last Bolton team to taste real success. It is true that Wanderers finished top of English football's second tier in 1978 and 1997 with attractive teams dear to the heart of almost every Bolton fan. And then there were the League Cup Final appearances of 1995 and 2004, plus two play-off triumphs and the heady days of European competition in the mid-Noughties. Who, for instance, could forget that freezing night in Bavaria when Bolton held the Bayern Munich of Ribery, Schweinsteiger, Podolski and Kahn to 2-2 with a back four which read McCann, O'Brien, Michalik and Cid? Not me, for sure, even though the memory is filtered through a veil of Bavarian beer!

Yet for all those memorable moments, the fact remains that the last time Bolton won one of the three major domestic trophies was at Wembley on May 3rd 1958 with a team exclusively recruited for £10 signing-on fees, five of whose surnames began with the letter 'H' including the 26-year-old right full-back, Hartle. The reverence with which the 1958 team is still held in Bolton reflects that success and this memoir will, I hope, be some kind of tribute to those players.

But there's more to Roy's story than Wembley 1958, important as it is. For instance how many Englishmen can boast that they coached someone who went on to manage a World Cup winning team? Well, there's at least one – and he's the subject of this biography.

Whose Midlands family was so large and the age range so diverse that he has a nephew who is eight months older than him?

And whose wife once turned down Sir Stanley Matthews as a candidate for her husband's testimonial side with the words, "I think he's got a full team"? The notion of the great Matthews waiting head bowed like a small boy in the playground while lesser talents are picked ahead of him is irresistible. Thankfully it can be reported that Sir Stan *was* chosen eventually and, at the age of fifty-four, provided excellent entertainment for the crowd at Roy's 1969 testimonial match which ended on a crowd-pleasing score of 10-9.

While we have Matthews in mind, the record books note that in the Coronation year of 1953 Roy played for Bolton in an FA Cup thriller which ended with the memorable score of 4-3. Sadly for Roy, the match was not the famous Cup Final of that year but the semi at Maine Road against Everton in which the Toffees, 4-0 down at half time, mounted a spirited recovery to nearly level the match. Bolton hung on and went through to Wembley to face Blackpool, Stan Matthews and the fans of every team in the country, bar one. But, by the time that celebrated match came around Roy, who had played in every FA Cup tie during his debut season, was out of the side, dropped without explanation. Disappointment over the snub would linger with him throughout his career and beyond.

You need to be tough to deal with a setback like that and they don't come much tougher than Roy Hartle as many an aging left-winger will still testify with a shudder. But there was more to Roy than the sight and sound of prancing wingers being unceremoniously dumped down the grass slope and on to the gravel at Burnden Park. No less an authority on full-backs than Jimmy Armfield makes the point that Roy really could play and was unlucky not to win an international cap or two like Tommy Banks, his partner in Bolton's most celebrated full-back double act. Having said that, there's no doubt that Roy is right up at the top in the pantheon of football's legendary hard men!

All that toughness and determination was needed in 2007 after Roy suffered a severe stroke which paralysed him down his left side, put him into a wheelchair and impaired his memory. It was a devastating blow to a man who had always been fit and alert and who embodied the qualities of strength and physical presence. But, with stalwart help from Barbara, Roy fought back from this terrible blow and surprised many people with the extent of his recovery.

While this is a memoir about a football legend and a bygone age, it is also, in part, a personal story. For a few years near the end of Roy's career our paths crossed briefly, although of course he never knew anything about it. Along with Wyn Davies, Francis Lee, Freddie Hill and Eddie Hopkinson, Roy was one of my earliest footballing heroes.

And when I came to write his story I found out that our links went back even further than that. For, when I was very young, Roy lived in the very next cobbled street to ours in the glowering shadow of the huge cotton mill where my Dad had once worked!

Even without those connections I would have jumped at the chance to write the biography of one of my home town's heroes. As it is I'm honoured to have been asked to set down Roy's story. Because, above all, I am a fan.

1

COUNTRY BUMPKIN

It is a grim freezing cold Saturday afternoon at Burnden Park in the early Sixties, well before the permissive society has made its debut or is even a gleam in the eye of anyone around these parts. Clinging on to the navy blue wooden slatted fence at the point where the Great Lever End bends round towards the Burnden Paddock are a ragged bunch of urchin school kids. Noses run and fingers lose feeling as each boy silently curses that he is not brave enough to ignore the inevitable taunts and put on the woollen gloves that a thoughtful mum has stuffed into the pockets of his gabardine mac. The less committed tear around madly in the empty space between the fence and where the worn terracing with its concrete and metal stanchions begins. But most of the boys take note of what is happening on the other side of the fence with interest and occasional enthusiasm. They watch delightedly as fiery Bolton Wanderers goalkeeper Eddie Hopkinson hands out his routine bollockings to an erring defence – even when the error is plainly his fault. "First thing they told me when I got into the team," said left-back that day Syd Farrimond, "was whatever happens if they've scored a goal don't turn round because if you do Hoppy will be at you saying it's your fault." Those freezing kids also bet each other how long it will be before lanky centre-half Bryan Edwards has blood streaming down his face after a typically robust aerial challenge. "Slim would have stitches in his eyebrows every week," marvelled Edwards' good pal and Syd's predecessor as Wanderers left back, Tommy Banks.

But today most of those kids aren't bothered at all about Hoppy's tantrums or Slim's chance of finishing Saturday out of hospital. Instead they are gazing in awe at Tommy's erstwhile and Syd's current full back partner, Roy "Chopper" Hartle - and it's because of something astonishing that has just happened right in front of them.

Roy Hartle has no need of gloves or gabardine as he faces today's left-winger, short-sleeved white shirt tight to his frame, dark hair immaculately swept back from his high forehead and a menacing glint in his eye. The identity of the opponent doesn't really matter - they're all "yellow-bellies" anyway according to Tommy Banks - but whoever he is this guy has the ball and Roy is about six or seven feet away standing absolutely still, left foot in front of right, daring him to try to take it on the outside. Understandably the winger, heavily into self-preservation, doesn't much fancy laying himself open to a bone-jarring challenge so, without more ado, he crosses the ball. His kick, however, while powerful is misdirected and instead of threatening Hoppy's goal, it flies smack into Roy's face. Hard enough to pole-axe a charging rhino. And, instead of collapsing like a blancmange and rolling around in agony, Roy just remains standing, still staring intently at the ball which has landed straight back at the kicker's feet. The shocked winger takes one look at the ball and another into Roy's ice-cold assassin's eyes – and then throws himself down the banking onto the red shale track so as to cut out the middle man. OK, that final bit doesn't happen but even if it had, none of those watching kids would have noticed. They are all still staring at Roy, marvelling at how he has not even flinched as the heavy, sodden, leather ball smashes into his face from just a few feet away. Any one of them in that position would have instinctively turned away and allowed the ball to hit his back. Even most professional full-backs would find it difficult not to shy away as the ball hurtled towards them. Yet Roy is still impressively immobile, the only evidence of what has just happened being the large circular muddy mark around his left eye. It is the equivalent of cricket's hard man of that era, Brian Close, fielding at short leg and not turning a hair as the batsman sweeps the ball at his head.

Where did such toughness originate? Surely Roy was hewn from the same Lancashire coal seam as his old full-back partner Banky or big mate Nat Lofthouse, both proud former pitmen. But no. Surprisingly Roy Hartle is a self-confessed country bumpkin, whose antecedents spring from rural communities in the shadow of Worcestershire's Malvern Hills, which so inspired the uplifting music of that most English of composers, Edward Elgar. So, far from the Hartle family tree sprouting out of industrial areas like Tyldesley, Daubhill or Farnworth, it's full of quaint names like Upton Warren, Wychbold and Pershore, small villages that speak of a more gentle, less frenetic, almost pre-industrial England.

It is just beyond these rolling hills a few miles further north towards Roy's birthplace that we must look to begin to answer the question of what made him. At first glance, Catshill, the West Midlands village in which Leslie Roy Hartle was born on October 4th 1931, looks to begin to have the makings of an answer. This tiny haven is firmly trapped in the centre of a rectangle of major highways. In this bizarre transportation noose the M5 does a dog leg to provide two sides of the rectangle, the M42 is the base and up the east side stretches the A38 which links Birmingham eleven miles to the north and Worcester, a similar distance south. But these are modern highways, unheard of in the 1930s when Roy arrived on the scene. And even the notion of Catshill being throttled by the rush and roar of a modern traffic system fades gently away once you're in the middle of the noose. True, the motorways' grumbling presence is never far away. But, give or take a bunch of newer houses, the village is recognisably the same rural community three miles from Bromsgrove in which Roy grew up, the youngest of ten children.

A startling statistic to be sure but one not uncommon in that age of large families. Far more unusual is the age gap between Roy and most of his siblings. The oldest, Harry, born in 1905, was twenty-six when Roy arrived on the scene. The youngest, his sister Joan, was seven. His dad, Henry, or 'Ike' as he was known within the family, was eight years away from drawing his pension when Roy arrived and his mother Elizabeth was an exhausted forty-three year-old when she had her final child. Perhaps the most telling statistic is that Dennis Hartle, the son of second brother Len, is eight months older than his Uncle Roy!

It would be tempting at this point to devise a theory about how young Roy sowed the seeds of the hard man legend by being forced to stick up for himself amid a maelstrom of older sibling rivalry and simmering violence as he grew up at the small terraced cottage in Woodrow Lane, Catshill, into which they were all crammed. It would also be ridiculous. Roy's brothers, Harry, Len and nineteen-year-old Percy had already fled the nest. Of Roy's five sisters (a sixth, Ethel, died in infancy in 1923) only Joan was even close to him in age. The others Gladys, Helen, Elsie and Vera, were all aged between thirteen and nineteen and it beggars belief that these women, all of child-bearing age by the time Roy started school, would have done anything other than mother - rather than smother - the baby of the family.

Roy's wife Barbara can confirm this. She remembered that even in the early 1950s when she met him, his loving sisters would still fondly refer to "our Roy this or our Roy that."

So Roy's toughness must have originated elsewhere; maybe it was in the family's economic circumstances. Nephew Dennis, who lived round the corner in Cobnall Road, recalled that they were poorer than average. Roy's mother regularly took in washing from other villagers and, along with her daughters, helped the farmer across the road with seasonal pea and potato picking. Dad Ike was a railwayman, who would also give the same farmer a hand with his ploughing. However there's no suggestion that anyone in the family, least of all the baby of the brood, wanted for the basics of food, warmth and clothing.

Maybe Roy's toughness came from growing up in a 1930s community coarsened by depression and forced to live on its wits. Again this is far too simplistic. While money was undoubtedly tight in the region, the West Midlands coped with the great depression far better than the North West with its textiles and coal and the North East and its reliance on pits and ship yards. One of the reasons for the area's relative prosperity could be found at Austin's Longbridge plant six miles away from Catshill. Far from struggling, Austin was in profit for the whole of the 1930s due to the astonishing success of the mass produced Austin 7, or Baby Austin as it became known. And a good proportion of the Hartle family was employed in the motor industry. At various times Harry, Len, Gladys, Joan and her husband George all had jobs at Longbridge and Vera worked at BSA, in nearby Redditch, which made motorbikes. The tradition continued after the war when Roy briefly worked at Austin until he went into the Army and Dennis did forty years on the Longbridge production line. So, while money was tight, the Hartle family was certainly not on the breadline.

Perhaps the solution can be found just down Woodrow Lane, on a large field, inevitably known as the rec. It's covered with houses now and has been for many years, its streets named on a racecourse theme giving us, among others, Lingfield Walk and Aintree Close. But during the 1930s this open expanse was the theatre of dreams for lads from Catshill and beyond. Dennis recalled: "If you went down on the rec on a Saturday from dawn you'd probably have twenty-two a side. Roy was a big lad and he was always a good footballer. Mind you, he'd kick anything that moved as well. He was very robust."

Roy did not disagree with this assessment but put it down to the survival instinct. "It was either them hit me or me hit them," he said. "So I got in first and that's stuck with me ever since. You either got tough or went off. It was as simple as that. It never did me any harm." Whether it did other lads any harm is not recorded but it is clear that the single-mindedness which took Roy to the top of the game was at least partially forged in that hurly-burly on Catshill Rec.

Yet, in an echo of his dual personality of the future - hard man on the pitch, golden-voiced charmer off it - the lad who sorted them all out was a different prospect away from the playing field. Years later his mother Eliza told Barbara that Roy was a shy child. A "softy" in fact.

"He wouldn't go in people's houses when his Mum took him out," explained Barbara. "He'd sit on the doorstep until she came out." This compelling image of a shy and lonely little fellow, sucking his thumb on a well-scrubbed step will no doubt give pause for thought to those ageing left-wingers recalling long-faded bruises.

Strength and determination were not the only early pointers to Roy's eventual soccer successes. It was in his genes too. Dennis recalled that they would kick a tennis ball all the way to Catshill Primary School and back, a process which was as natural as breathing to both boys because sporting prowess ran in the Hartle family. "I had always wanted to be a footballer because my father was a footballer and my brothers were locally," Roy revealed. In fact his second brother Len had been given his own tantalising glimpse of a football career, only to have it snatched away by his father.

Dennis explained: "Notts County wanted my Dad to go for a trial but in those days money was tight and his Dad, Ike, said, 'no you can't go, you've got to stop here and earn your coppers'. He was a very good footballer, a half-back, two-footed as well."

Ike's old-fashioned no-nonsense approach to fatherhood may have contributed to toughening up his youngest son in yet another way. Explained Roy: "My Dad used to sit down on match day listening to the results on the radio and if you interrupted him it was a smack across the face. That was it, no talking." Luckily, by the time Roy was into his teens, Ike had mellowed enough to give the lad's blossoming football career his blessing – and to pass on some extremely useful advice. In the meantime older brother Len stayed in the area, winning trophies for the Catshill village team and turning out for Austin Aero where he worked on the aircraft production line.

The aircraft connection made the area a natural target for German bombers during the Second World War, with Catshill and the nearby town of Bromsgrove close enough to Longbridge to raise fears that short-sightedness among German pilots on raids during the winter of 1940 would impact on them. And on at least one occasion those worries were not misplaced. In the only daylight raid in the area during the war, a Heinkel bomber on its way back from a raid on Longbridge was engaged in a dogfight by three RAF Hurricane fighters over Bromsgrove Rovers' Victoria Ground, where Roy would later play junior and some senior football. Catshill too was not immune to attack. Dennis remembered that an explosion just down the road from Roy's house in Woodrow Lane killed a man outside his home.

Despite the excitement and fears heightened by air raids and anything else that Hitler was prepared to throw at him, young Roy had other matters on his mind. He was a decent pupil at Catshill Primary and later Catshill County Senior School as his report for the term ending July 1945 demonstrated. Phrases such as, "he has worked hard and made good progress," and "has the ability to do well," are sprinkled throughout the report. And while there are no 'A' grades in evidence, the report contains many a 'B' and 'B+' with only a couple of 'Cs'.

"I was good at one subject at school," he said rather modestly "and that was football." The maths teacher, Mr Gilbert, who doubled as the sports master, agreed that Roy was more adept at kicking than counting but there's a Catshill legend that Mr Gilbert once dropped Roy from the school team for not trying! Roy can't recall the incident but if true it was surely the first and only time it happened in his career.

Roy could also swing a mean cricket bat, turning out for the village's youth side, and demonstrating his ability to belt the ball a mighty distance. Oddly his form master Mr Cooke makes no mention of football in the school report but does confirm that Roy was "a keen cricketer and has done well for the school." But football was his passion and he soon had the medals to indicate he was on his way to higher things. In season 1947-48 Catshill Youth Team won the Kings Norton Under-21 League and Cup. "We had a really good side," says Dennis, who also turned out for the team. "There was only Roy who really made it from the team but we had a centre-forward who played for Alvechurch. We always thought he might make it but he never did."

One boy who was definitely on the verge of making it by then was Roy. At the end of the season that he won the double for Catshill, Roy had been spotted by Bolton. It was at a major Worcestershire county schoolboys match against Staffordshire at Bromsgrove Rovers and yet it was only by good fortune that he was seen at all.

Explained Dennis: "Roy should not have been playing that day. But one of the other players was taken ill and Roy took his place." Watching the match was a Wanderers scout with a famous name. Roy recalled: "It was a man called Mr Westwood. He was the uncle of the famous Ray Westwood that we had at Burnden in the Thirties and Forties. He came over and had a chat and he said would I like to sign for Bolton? So I came up and had a couple of trials and things worked out quite well."

However, Bolton was not the first club to show an interest in Roy. The local giants Birmingham, Wolves and Aston Villa, who noted his enthusiastic and committed performances at school and for Catshill and Bromsgrove Rovers Juniors, were all keen to sign him on amateur forms. Here, the advice of his Dad proved crucial.

Roy said: "My father said it might be better to go somewhere where you're not known rather than where you're a local lad who might get a bit more stick than someone from somewhere else. That was his advice. I took it and I've never regretted it."

Anyone who doubts that Ike's advice was spot-on should think back to the treatment Wanderers born locally have traditionally received. Before he became one of the best midfielders Bolton has ever had, Roy Greaves took his share of stick from a section of the Burnden crowd before settling into a successful career which propelled him to 17th spot in a table of Wanderers fifty top soccer legends – one place in front of another Roy, the subject of this biography. Another player born within the sound of Bolton Town Hall clock to be given disproportionately unjust treatment was Jimmy Phillips (37th place). And even the Wanderers' No 1 legend Nat Lofthouse took criticism from the terraces early in his career. Perhaps it is that crowds are so desperate for their own local lads to shine that they feel the disappointment all the more keenly when those players are not immediate successes.

Roy would have to wait nearly four years before stepping on to the Burnden pitch as a first team player to test his Dad's theory out. He even had to hang around for his first junior game, as after the successful trial and signing amateur forms for the club on November 15th 1948, he heard nothing more from the Wanderers over the Christmas period and into January.

"I began to get worried," he revealed. "I thought they must have so many players, they can't fit me in. So I wrote to the club. They explained that the grounds were bad and they didn't want me to make the trip only for my match to be called off."

Soon however Roy, carrying his boots in a small cardboard suitcase, was making the regular trip north and what a culture shock it proved to be for a kid brought up in a tiny community. "I was a country bumpkin," he admits. "There's no two ways about it. I hadn't really been out of the village – if we went to Bromsgrove it was like a day out. To think of going to a place like New Street Station in Birmingham and from there up to Manchester was another world. I used to come up into Manchester in the fog and the smog and the wet. Then I'd catch the bus and come to Bolton. It was another world and a frightening one at that."

Roy arrived in smoggy, foggy Bolton in February 1949, unable to pass his thanks on to Ray Westwood for his scouting uncle's crucial intervention. Westwood, perhaps the greatest Bolton player of the era that linked the 1920s triple FA Cup-winning side and the Lofthouse years, had been transferred to Chester in October 1947, ending a

Wanderers career which saw him score 144 goals in 333 appearances, a tally bettered only by Jack Milsom, David Jack, Joe Smith and Lofthouse himself.

                                ﻉ   ﻉ   ﻉ

It's somewhat odd that Bolton's most celebrated full back pairing teamed up for the first time not at Burnden Park but in rural Shropshire. When Roy arrived at the club as a lowly amateur, Tommy Banks had already made his professional first team debut and their paths never crossed – until they finally met on the parade ground.

In February 1950 Roy reported to Park Hall Camp, a mile east of the Shropshire market town of Oswestry, to begin his National Service. This two-year stint in the "Lads Army" was compulsory for young men aged between seventeen and thirty and since conscription ended in 1963 a number of myths have grown up about it. The most pervasive, repeated to my generation ad nauseum, by our elders and betters is that "it did you good" and would "teach layabouts like yourselves a thing or two about hard work and discipline" as if that were the very reason for its existence. In fact conscription was reintroduced in 1947 (having been discontinued at the end of the war) not through any desire to increase the moral fibre of Britain's juvenile delinquents but because it was the only way for the country to meet its overseas military commitments. At the time Britain was still considered a major player in international affairs.

And in a deliciously ironic response to the "hard work and discipline" brigade, it could be argued that far from producing a generation of order-obeying automatons, National Service actually hastened the arrival in British society of 'the teenager'. Social historian David Kynaston has written of "...the view that these two years spent

EARLY BALL . . .
even as a toddler Roy was into
football.

LITTLE ANGEL . . .

Roy as a very smart . . . .
old.

MUM ELIZABETH who
was forty-three when her
10th child Roy was born.

ROY'S DAD HENRY
or 'Ike' as he was known to the
family

FAMILY GUY . . . Roy, aged 11 with his
niece Sheila, the daughter of his eldest
sister Gladys.

*FIRST TEAM ...
the Catshill Primary
School XI of 1943-
44. Roy is far left on
the back row and his
nephew Dennis is
second right on the
same row.*

HARD-HITTER ...

*Roy (middle row, right)
with team-mates in the
Catshill village cricket
team.*

*ROY (above left) became so fit and
strong during National Service ...*

*... that he could balance
two boys sitting on a plank
across his shoulders!*

as involuntary conscripts with a bunch of other 18 and 19-year-olds provided a shared experience – living away from home, going out together to pubs, dance halls and so on without any parental restraint – that did much to accelerate the arrival of 'youth' as a category in its own right."

Another myth was that peacetime conscripts faced no dangers – and it's true most didn't. But during the period of National Service there were emergencies in Malaya, Cyprus, Suez and Kenya. And in the months after Roy received his call-up papers in one of those familiar brown envelopes, the place where National Servicemen least wanted to find themselves was Korea. Some had to be there, however. Between April 22nd and 25th 1951, conscripts in the Gloucester Regiment took part in the Battle of the Imjin River, near Seoul. The regiment was surrounded by Chinese forces on Hill 235 (later known as Gloster Hill) and suffered over 600 casualties including 500 captured as prisoners of war.

Tommy Banks remembered that most of the lads he trained with from January 1951 went off to Korea while he stayed at Oswestry as a Physical Training Instructor. Although Banky could not be sure of their fate, he said: "I never saw any of them again."

Eleven months before this Roy had arrived at Park Hall Camp, as 22331915 Gunner Hartle, if not quite as nervous as when he stepped off the train in Bolton for the first time, then apprehensive enough. He could not know that, despite losing two important years of his early football career, his stint in the military would be the making of him. "I did enjoy it," he said. "It made a man of me and I blossomed during it."

But before that he and the other nervous lads getting off the train at Gobowen Station had to get used to the sheer size of the place. At the time Park Hall had around two thousand young recruits about to do their basic training and there was a new intake every fortnight. And at first the seemingly endless square bashing, polishing and gym work were punishing – even for a fit young footballer. "It was hard work," admitted Roy, "harder than I ever thought it would have been."

Luckily his footballing prowess had already marked him out as special in the eyes of an influential figure. The Regimental Sergeant Major, a Welshman, had spotted a likely recruit for the regiment's team. Roy explained: "After basic training you'd usually be sent to another camp but he told me, 'You're not going anywhere else'. He was nutty about football."

In fact Roy was going somewhere else but it would only be to Aldershot for training to become a Physical Training Instructor, or PTI. When he returned to Oswestry six weeks later, he was leaner, fitter and ready to take on his duties as a lance corporal with 17 Training Regiment Royal Artillery, tasks which as well as training the new recruits would include playing right back and centre half for the regiment. Being taller than average, Roy was also reckoned by the top brass to be a basketball star in the making despite never having played the game before. This potential was soon realised too as he quickly progressed from the regimental team to full Army representative honours. Tommy Banks recalled that: "Roy was a top-notch basketball player. He was a big lad and good in defence."

But it was his defensive prowess with a football which really stood out. Each regimental side was allowed six professionals and five amateurs and 17 Training not only had Roy as an amateur but also centre half Jimmy Dugdale who went on to pick up FA Cup winner's medals in 1954 for West Brom and 1957 for Aston Villa. In fact everyone bar the goalkeeper was on the books of a professional club and it was hardly surprising that the 17 Training team was all-conquering. The following season, by which time Tommy had arrived on the scene, they were the top team in Western Command. Both Roy and Tommy also played for Western Command, a team good enough to beat the Northern Irish League side 4-2 in 1952. Roy had left the army by then, but coincidentally would play against the Northern Irish League in 1958 - his only professional representative game.

The arrival of Tommy at Oswestry in January 1951 had put Roy in something of a dilemma. On the one hand he was an established PTI, a 'lance jack' whose confidence had grown enormously in the preceding eleven months. On the other he was an amateur who had played only junior football for Bolton Wanderers. By contrast new squaddie Tommy Banks had made his Wanderers first team professional debut nearly three years before in April 1948. And Roy freely admitted he was in awe of the new boy.

Tommy remembers just after arriving at Park Hall Camp being approached by Roy. "He came to me and said, 'Do you play for the Wanderers?' and I said, 'Aye I do.' He said, 'I've signed amateur forms and I'm hoping to go when I've finished.' He had twelve months to do by then."

If that sounds confident enough from Roy then listen to his version. "I'd never met Tom before," he said, "and I thought how do I address him? I'm a young kid who's played in the A, B, and C teams and this man's actually played in the first team and it worried me. I was a PTI corporal ... and he was a squaddie. I can remember going up to him and I was in awe. This sounds absolutely stupid but I was. I'd never met a pro like Banky who'd played in the First Division."

However, Roy's sense of awe did not last too long as, when push came to shove, Tommy was just one of a new intake dressed in an ill-fitting great coat. During National Service new boys were not exactly measured for their uniforms – they got whatever was going. Lance Corporal Hartle explained: "Tom has rather long arms and, he won't mind me saying this, quite short legs. He stood there on parade and his overcoat was up on his elbow and it's dragging on the floor. I went up to him and had a chat and thought, 'He's not that frightening when he looks like that.'"

Tommy's first views of his new colleague were equally unflattering. He said: "Roy was the funniest PTI you'll ever see. He couldn't even do a forward roll – but he was good at basketball." By this time Tommy was a PTI too after six weeks training with the gang of lads many of whom would soon be on their way to Korea. However, before he could join Roy in the gym putting the recruits through their paces Tommy had to overcome an awkward piece of bureaucracy. "I'd volunteered for the Paratroops," he revealed, "and the major said they should let me go." Luckily, like Roy before him Tommy was seen by the Welsh RSM as a huge potential asset to the sporting ambitions of the regiment and his brief flirtation with the Paras was conveniently kicked into the long grass.

As well as training the new boys both Roy and Tommy took full advantage of the gym facilities on offer and came to consider themselves more as sportsmen rather than soldiers. Roy said: "For two years we were professional athletes almost because we were in the gym all day long, enjoying ourselves organising five-a-sides and eleven-a-sides."

It was during these games that Roy came up against another Royal Artilleryman who showed him how far he needed to develop to become a professional footballer.

Tommy Taylor arrived at Oswestry three months after Roy

in May 1950 and just a few months before he made his debut for Barnsley. By May 1953, a couple of months after he'd signed for Manchester United for a pound under £30,000, Taylor would make his debut for England and eventually replace Nat Lofthouse as England's first-choice centre forward. So not a bad benchmark to test yourself against! Roy said: "I played against Tommy Taylor and if you're playing with or against players like that you soon pick up the ropes. It was really good. And that's when I blossomed. I wasn't good enough before that. Tommy was a great player. Unbelievable, absolutely unbelievable!"

Of course there was still soldiering to do. Every week the PTIs had to supervise a five-mile march for the recruits who were passing out – often literally. Roy and Banky were on hand to pick up the kit these exhausted kids had discarded. Tommy explained: "Sometimes we had six rifles and four kit bags apiece because they were getting knackered as they came around. It was only a five-mile march but these lads had never done anything like that. Before we got back to the barracks we'd give all the kit back to them or there'd be hell to pay."

For all that they were regularly staggering around with the discarded equipment from unfit kids, it wasn't a bad life. Indeed Roy considered making soldiering his profession when his military stint came to an end in February 1952. "I was tempted to stay on in the Army," he said. "I could have pursued it as a career." But although he remained a reservist liable for recall at any time until November 1955, Roy's military career was effectively over.

That he didn't continue as a solider can be put down to the interest shown by two First Division clubs who wanted his signature on a professional contract. One naturally enough was the club for which Roy had joined as an amateur in 1948 – Bolton Wanderers.

The other was one of the Midlands clubs who'd tried to sign him as a schoolboy. Indeed, it's a bizarre fact that both members of Bolton's most famous full-back pairing could have been turning out together for an altogether different Wanderers. Wolves had come in for Tommy after he'd made his debut for Bolton against them in April 1948 while still working at Mosley Common Colliery, near Tyldesley. He turned them down despite a promise from the Wolves scout that the club would find him a pit job in the Midlands. And as we've already seen Roy rejected overtures from the Black Country on the advice of his Dad. Tommy would be approached again by Wolves as he came to the end of his National Service in 1953 after impressing for 17 Training Regiment's team against Wolves Reserves. The scout who showed interest was the same man who had tried to get him to sign five years before. And, by the time Tommy Banks rejected the men from Molineux a second time, Roy Hartle had already begun to establish himself at Bolton Wanderers.

2

MAKING A MARK

As Roy contemplated whether - and with which club - to turn professional it's worth examining the state football was in both nationally and locally at that time. In February 1952 England was still convinced it ruled the football world even though there had been a traumatic puncturing of that confidence during the 1950 World Cup in Brazil, the first time England had entered the competition. Lining up against a bunch of part-timers from the USA, England, who included Stan Mortensen, Tom Finney and Wilf Mannion (Stanley Matthews was being rested for later stages that England unfortunately would not see) managed to lose the game 1-0. The result was so unexpected that a story went around that the score transmitted over the wires was a misprint and England had in fact won 10-1. This tale turned out to be untrue but the fact that it has been repeated ever since indicates just how shocking the result was. However, as England had laid siege to the USA goalmouth and hit the post and crossbar a number of times, once the shock had worn off the nation settled down to treat the defeat as just one of those things that happened from time to time, even to the best of teams.

And if results are anything to go by England were, at that time, one of the best teams around. In thirty post-war matches up to then, England had won twenty-three, drawn three and lost four. The victories included a 10-0 thrashing of Portugal in Lisbon in May 1947 and the 2-0 defeat of Italy in November 1949 at White Hart Lane. In a five-day period just six weeks before that USA defeat in

Belo Horizonte, England beat Portugal and Belgium away, 5-3 and 4-0 respectively. To add to the confidence that our island's football really was superior to the rest, one of those three England defeats was the 3-1 reverse against Scotland at Wembley in April 1949.

The perceived invincibility of British football over its European counterparts could not have been more emphatically illustrated by something that had happened a year before Ray Westwood's uncle was spotting young Roy Hartle's potential in that Worcestershire Schools trial match.

Two weeks before England put ten past Portugal, a Great Britain Team took on The Rest of Europe. The match, on May 10th 1947 in front of 134,000 spectators at Hampden Park, Glasgow, was organised to celebrate the end of the Second World War and mark the re-admittance into FIFA of England, Wales and Scotland. The sports writer Frank Butler left readers in no doubt what was expected of our boys. After proclaiming that Britain Must Beat Europe, Butler declared that even a draw, "would be regarded as a moral victory by the continentals and leave us the laughing stock of Europe." Butler added that The Rest of Europe squad had, "Cleverly avoided revealing any of their talents to the British reporters who watched them yesterday. All they showed was some mighty fine acrobatics and high kicking." So we were up against a team of cunning clowns and show girls. What could possibly go wrong?

Well, in the end, nothing. Great Britain, with Matthews sparkling on the right wing steamrollered The Rest of Europe 6-1, a victory which included goals from Mannion, Tommy Lawton and Billy Steel. A bullish Butler concluded that "Europe is now convinced that the British are now the bosses of Soccer." We were top dogs and nothing would knock us off our perch - not even the USA's fluky victory in

1950. Nothing at all - until the Hungarians led by Ferenc Puskas came calling in November 1953.

If British football was in the ascendancy as the Forties became the Fifties then matters at Bolton were looking up as well. While Roy was still developing his football skills and fitness in the Army, Bill Ridding, who had been chief trainer to the England team at the Brazil World Cup, was given the job of Bolton manager on a permanent basis in February 1951. He and newly appointed trainer, the respected disciplinarian, tactician and former Wanderers player George Taylor, steered the club into an eighth place finish in Division One, a considerable improvement on the previous four seasons when Wanderers had finished no higher than fourteenth.

Ridding stayed on as manager during my childhood and adolescence and throughout Roy's career with the club, until 1968. He looked a bit like a bemused accountant who'd wandered into Burnden Park by mistake but this appearance was deceptive. Ridding had had a promising early career as a centre forward with Tranmere Rovers and Manchester United cut short by a knee injury when he was twenty-four. This setback turned out to be a stroke of luck for Bolton as, after serving as physiotherapist and then trainer, he led the Wanderers through some of the club's most successful years.

His appointment as Bolton manager, however, left him understandably apprehensive and he later revealed: "I thought that I may have left my true vocation behind because I enjoyed being a trainer ... but gradually I got over the manager's growing pains and in the end I couldn't see myself doing anything else."

He soon set about building for success and at the end of his first full season in charge, 1951-52, the club finished in fifth place in Division One, Bolton's best post-war performance up to that point.

Along the way, they notched up Burnden Park's biggest post-war league crowd of 55,477 whilst beating Manchester United 1-0 and Ridding paid out a club record fee of £27,000 to sign Harold Hassall from Huddersfield Town and complete an all-international forward line for the team which also included Billy Hughes, Willie Moir, Nat Lofthouse and Bobby Langton.

The season had one more bonus for Wanderers fans. On May 25th 1952 Lofthouse, who had made his England debut in November 1950, earned the title that would define him to the sporting public and beyond for the rest of his life. Playing for England against an Austria side reckoned to be the most powerful in Europe, the Bolton man showed his trademark determination and courage, scoring two goals in a 3-2 victory. The second of these, which turned out to be a last-minute winner, came after Nat collected a pass from Tom Finney and was tripped and hacked at in a forty-yard run before being involved in a sickening collision with the Austrian goalkeeper Josef Musil, which didn't stop him steering the ball into the net. Unfortunately the impact did prevent Nat seeing the results of his bravery.

"I had mixed feelings about it ... as I was carried off on a stretcher," Nat wrote later. "But after treatment from our trainer Jimmy Trotter I went back on ... and what's more I hit the upright before the end of the game." England manager Walter Winterbottom was quick to describe Lofty's winner as "a wonderful solo goal", something with which the thousands of National Servicemen in the Austrian capital that day would agree as they chaired off the newly designated Lion of Vienna.

Not long after Harold Hassall arrived at Burnden Ridding made a less exalted signing but one that would prove more far-reaching for the club. On February 25th, 1952, Roy Hartle put pen to paper on a professional deal which would see him earn £5 a week and become the proud recipient of a pair of old-fashioned football boots from Albert Ward's sports shop in Bradshawgate. These had to last the whole of the season.

"They were real over-the-ankle things," said Roy. "And by the time the season was halfway over they were awful. You couldn't have another pair either. You had to put your feet in a bucket of water to soften the leather because it was really thick."

Yet, when he arrived at Burnden, it wasn't football boots that were Roy's immediate problem but other footballers. On signing full professional forms he found to his dismay that the place was crawling with professional full-backs.

"It wasn't a big squad," he said, "but for some unknown reason they'd got seven full-time full-backs ... and I made the eighth. Now there's only four teams. There's the first team, there's the reserves, the A and the B team so there's two professional full-backs for each team and I'm obviously in the B team. I thought, 'I'm never going to break through.' "

It was a problem that would have tested the confidence of any new boy but luckily this period of self-doubt did not last long. For one thing, although he was a new pro, Roy was as fit as anybody on the staff. Those five and eleven-a-sides at Oswestry had done their job and the fact that he hadn't been shown up against future stars like Tommy Taylor in regimental games had boosted his confidence. Moreover, when he considered the obstacles to his passage into the first team, Roy quickly decided that they were not as insurmountable as he'd first imagined.

He said: "I looked at one or two of the pros and thought, 'He's not much better than me really. He can play better than me but I've got that little bit more determination and want to be a good player' so yeah, I've got a chance."

His optimism was well-founded as within four days of signing on as a professional, Roy was already in the Reserves. On March 1st 1952 he played in the Central League side which won 2-0 at Villa Park. By the end of the month he was attracting attention not just for his trademark muscular play but his distribution skills in serving up decent passes to the forwards. They included Ray Parry, back in the Reserves after his first-team debut at the age of fifteen years and 267 days – making him the youngest player ever to turn out for the Wanderers.

Roy continued to catch the eye with his Central League performances for the rest of the season and it seemed only a matter of time before his chance came to step up into the seniors. That opportunity arrived in the following 1952-53 campaign.

3

FINAL INSULT

One match in his debut season casts a long shadow over Roy's career and later life and it's a game in which he didn't play – although he did receive a medal for it. That match is one of the best-known and most talked about English domestic games ever. Any short pen picture of Roy Hartle invariably mentions that, after playing in every round of the FA Cup including the dramatic semi at Maine Road, he was left out of the Cup Final team. It's a decision that still bugged him sixty years later, particularly due to the fact that he claims that the manager Bill Ridding didn't tell him why he was being dropped before the Wanderers' biggest post-war game to date.

"I managed every round in '53, up to and including the semi and then was left out of the Final team. I couldn't believe I'd been dropped," he said, still sounding bemused. "I mean, I'd played in every game."

Yet a closer examination reveals that the axing was not as unambiguously brutal as it first seems. For a start, as the Final approached, Roy's form had begun to suffer to the extent that he had been out of the first team for four matches before the Wembley showpiece. For another, the man who replaced him was vastly more experienced.

That is not to play down Roy's dismay – it was undoubtedly a shattering blow to a 21-year-old. But the fact is that as Wembley loomed he was in a position that fifteen months before would have been inconceivable to him. At that time he'd been grateful to play his first game in the Reserves and not disgrace himself. And nine months later Ridding had decided that Roy's consistency for the second string merited a chance to show what he could do in the first team.

That opportunity was to come on Boxing Day 1952 – only to be snatched away. Bolton had lost a 6-4 thriller to Arsenal at Burnden on Christmas Day but the players of both clubs were all-too aware that there was no chance of putting their feet up by the festive fire that evening. Instead, amazing as it sounds these days, both the Wanderers and Gunners squads had to pile straight on to the London train for a return match at Highbury - the following day!

Mince pies and mulled wine would have been the last thing on Roy's mind, anyway. He had already been told that he was to replace the regular right-back John Ball, whose form had dipped. But Roy's feelings of delight mixed with nervousness were shattered the following morning when the Arsenal match was called off due to a heavy London fog. It meant he had a nervous six-day wait for his first team debut which finally came at Burnden Park on January 1st 1953 against Charlton Athletic.

Some professionals will tell you that they remember every kick of their first match. Many more, however, admit that their debut went by in a complete blur. Roy's experience falls definitely into the second category. While agreeing it was "a fabulous day", he admits that the match, which Wanderers lost 2-1, passed in a flash. Yet he does have one memory of the occasion which evocatively captures the particular time and which could never happen today.

Roy explained: "On Christmas Day, Boxing Day and New Year's Day ... you'd always get the smell of the little cigars everybody had at Christmas because no-one smoked cigars the rest of the year but everybody had a cigar at Christmas time. We used to run out on

Burnden from the moat up on to the pitch and you could smell this aroma going round, this nice cigar thing which always sticks in your mind."

Despite the tobacco clouds this particular match was not fogged off and Roy left the pitch to congratulations and hand-shakes from his team mates. The local paper too had been impressed and gave the opinion that it had been "a very encouraging first appearance." The report went on: "The heavy pitch suited his weighty build better than a fast dry one would be likely to, but he nevertheless held his own against the mercurial Kiernan and was going better the longer play lasted."

The Bolton Evening News was not exaggerating the credentials of Roy's first senior opponent either, as that "mercurial" left-winger Billy Kiernan was one of Charlton's best-ever players. In an eleven-year career, Kiernan became the London club's seventh highest goal scorer of all time - pretty decent going for a winger - and was reckoned unlucky to have won only England B honours.

A couple of days after his debut, in a match against Blackpool, Roy showed the Burnden crowd another feature of his play that was to become a Hartle trademark when he made several vital clearances off the line with his goalkeeper Stan Hanson beaten. Bolton's 4-0 win that day surely boded well should the clubs meet later in the season.

Roy was now firmly part of the team and embarked on a run of twenty-four consecutive league and cup matches – a sequence which only ended three weeks before the Cup Final.

Similar weather to his scheduled league debut also put paid to Roy's first FA Cup game. The Third Round match against Fulham at Burnden was due to be played on Saturday January 10th but a smoke-filled fog settled over the whole town like a grubby blanket and the match was played the following Wednesday, when goals from Doug Holden, Moir and Lofthouse sealed a 3-1 victory. It took Bolton three games to get past Notts County in the Fourth Round – no such things as penalty shoot-outs in those days. The second replay against County at Hillsborough was settled by a single strike from Lofthouse, who would also provide the only goals in the next two cup games, against Luton and Third Division Gateshead who put up a stirring Sixth Round fight on their own ground.

Cup fever had really began to exert its grip on Boltonians before this game and ten trains carried ten thousand fans up to the North East after crowd scenes at Trinity Street Station, reminiscent of the start of Bolton Holidays. However, the lower league side put up a gallant display, ensuring for the Bolton defence at least that this was no grand day out. Just Malcolm Barrass among the defenders escaped criticism, of which Roy took a large share. "The only weakness in the winning side," according to the Evening News, "was in the back division where both Hartle and (left-back George) Higgins took half a game to gain anything like full composure." It was the first hint that Roy's continuing presence in the team might not be a foregone conclusion.

Other league highlights of Roy's opening spell in the first team included a 2-1 home victory against Manchester United. And five matches into the run, down at Portsmouth, Roy and Tommy Banks played together for the first time, although oddly not as full-back partners.

While Banky wore the number three shirt he was to make his own the following season, Roy replaced the injured Barrass at centre half with John Ball coming in for a single game at right back. The Hartle-Banks full-back pairing was first seen in a goalless draw at Liverpool at the beginning of March but the combination lasted just another two games, whereupon established left back Higgins reclaimed the number three shirt for one game before Tommy's older brother Ralph was drafted in for most of the remaining matches including the Cup Final. Still, it seems inconceivable that the celebrated Roy Hartle-Tommy Banks partnership would not resume for another two-and-a-half years.

The highlight of Roy's first run in the team was the FA Cup Semi-Final victory against Everton in front of seventy-five thousand spectators at Maine Road. In a mirror image of what was to happen in the Final, the match finished 4-3 to Bolton with goals from Lofthouse (2), Moir and Holden. However, those bald facts hardly tell the whole story as Wanderers had gone in at half time 4-0 up only to see the Toffees storm back in the second half and nearly draw level. After Everton's Tom Eglington had missed a penalty, Roy's despairing goal-line dive could not stop a header from John Parker going in and Peter Farrell further reduced the deficit with a shot from outside the area after a short free kick. Roy was then comprehensively beaten in the air by Everton's powerful centre forward Dave Hickson and the ball looped over to Parker who headed his second. However, Bolton's embattled defence hung on to take the Wanderers through to their first FA Cup Final for twenty-four years.

Roy played a further six league games after the semi and, while he was praised for his performance against Spurs at Burnden in early April, the writing was definitely on the wall. After a desperate away draw against Sheffield Wednesday a week later, there were newspaper plaudits for Hanson, Barrass, Ralph Banks, Bryan Edwards and Matthew McIlwaine – virtually the whole defence – but no mention of Roy, whose chances of Wembley glory were beginning to evaporate.

And, in a grim piece of symmetry, he was dropped for the rescheduled away match against Arsenal on April 15th, the very game in which he had been listed to make a Boxing Day debut.

So, seventeen days before the Cup Final, Bill Ridding restored John Ball to the team for the last four matches of the league campaign. This alerted Roy that his presence in the Final was anything but a formality, emphasised by Ball's improving form which shone through in the final league match of the season, a 3-2 away win against Newcastle.

Nevertheless when the Wembley team sheet went up three days before the Final with Ball's name inked in at right-back, Roy was devastated. While admitting that he did not consider himself a better player than Ball, who had been an understudy to the Irish star Johnny Carey at Old Trafford, he declared: "I couldn't believe I'd been dropped. I mean, I played in every game up to the Final."

Nephew Dennis also remembered how devastated he had been. "Roy was very, very upset about being left out," he confirmed.

Tommy Banks' assessment is typically more direct and hard-headed although he does have sympathy for Roy. "In his last two or three games, Roy couldn't kick the ball – he'd lost form," said Banky who added, however, that he didn't think that the senior professionals necessarily helped a young player who had lost confidence. Contrasting their attitudes with the togetherness of the 1958 team, Tommy described his experiences of that earlier FA Cup side with the comment: "When I got in the team it took them all their time to speak to you. We couldn't even train with the senior players."

About the club's choice of right back for the Final, Haydn Berry wrote: "In three league games since resuming, Ball has shown that he has recovered the confidence and workmanlike style that marked his earlier displays for the club and his greater experience weighted the scales in his favour over the strapping Bromsgrove back Roy Hartle. Manager Ridding told me that the matter had been fully and gravely discussed with every consideration for the fact that Hartle has played in every round to the Final. In omitting him the directors appreciated Hartle's position and inevitable sense of disappointment but felt they must go all out for the soundest side on form."

However, the move did not go down well with some fans, who vented their displeasure in the letters page of the Bolton Evening News. Fred Crompton, of Birley Street, Bolton, reckoned: "The so-called full-back problem for Saturday did not exist. Hartle and Higgins, (who had played against Luton, Gateshead and Everton) the men who helped take Wanderers to the final should be there – unless injured." It was followed by a note from the editor who admitted the paper had received a number of other letters protesting against the exclusion of Hartle and Higgins.

For Roy there was the scant consolation of being named as twelfth man, which involved getting measured up for a suit from Jacksons the Tailors and travelling down to London's Hendon Hall Hotel on the coach with the chosen team plus reserves George Higgins, Ray Parry and half-back Tommy Neill. He was also given a full Wembley kit which is on display to this day in the Roy Hartle Suite at the Reebok Stadium. However, possibly the only advantage of being twelfth man was that Roy never actually had to wear the kit, which six decades later is still beautifully shiny because, significantly for Wanderers' chances that day, it is made from silk. As a material silk breathes nowhere near as well as cotton so, as the players sweated on that sweltering May afternoon, their shirts retained the moisture, became heavier and contributed to their tiredness in the crucial last twenty minutes. It is significant that in their next Cup Final five years later, Bolton insisted on wearing cotton shirts - as Blackpool had done in 1953.

As to the famous match itself, Roy's nephew thinks the result could have been different if his younger relative had been in the team. "I always say that if he'd have been playing there was a good chance that Bolton would have won that match," suggested Dennis, "because I couldn't see the Blackpool left-winger Perry getting through to cross the ball for the last goal. I mean, I'm biased but I think Roy would have given him a bit of gravel rash."

Dennis's loyalty to Roy disguises the fact that it was Stan Matthews who crossed the ball for Bill Perry to score the last-gasp winner to make the score 4-3 and we'll never know whether Roy would have got in the way to deny the South African his place in sporting history. Even if Roy had been playing, however, there's no doubt he would have increasingly been a spectator as most of the trouble came down Bolton's left flank. Blackpool had already decided that Matthews against Ralph Banks was their likeliest avenue to success, a likelihood which increased dramatically with a first half injury to Bolton's left-half Eric Bell. Despite inside forward Harold Hassall dropping back to ably assist his full back, Blackpool were able to pour their efforts down that flank. Even when the injured Bell put Bolton 3-1 up with a header (Lofthouse and Moir were the other two Bolton scorers thanks to comedy goalkeeping by Blackpool's George Farm - to equal Hanson's fumbling efforts as Stan Mortensen scored the Seasiders' second) Blackpool, prompted by Ernie Taylor and Matthews, always looked likely to drag things back. And in the last twenty minutes, with Banks suffering from cramp and the Wanderers' sweat-sodden silk shirts getting heavier and heavier, the Seasiders did just that, culminating in Mortensen's late equaliser and Perry's last-gasp winner.

Afterwards the man from The Times could hardly contain his admiration for the 38-year-old Wizard of Dribble. "Matthews is a superb artist," he gushed, "a football genius beyond compare. He paints, as it were, in water colours and not oils. His work always has had that beautiful bloom that oils cannot give. He has it within him to turn mice into horses and nothing into everything. Now in those last 25 minutes he turned Blackpool into giants ..." Against nine fit men as well!

It took former Sheffield Wednesday centre forward Derek Dooley, who had recently been forced to retire from football after a serious injury, to put matters into some perspective. Dooley pointed to the debilitating effect that Bell's injury had had on Bolton, who "had to concentrate their efforts on the right wing and down the middle ... Bell could never hobble back fast enough to help in hampering Matthews. This threw extra work on Harold Hassall who did really well as an emergency left-half."

And, while not denying Matthews his eventual plaudits, Haydn Berry also lent the occasion a greater sense of reality. He wrote: "Matthews' performance should be considered in relation to the weakness of the opposition. He only ran away with the defence when the Bolton team was crippled and produced nothing wonderful before that. But the ball-holding powers that he possesses and his skill in 'drawing' a defence to him before crossing the vital pass, definitely turned defeat into victory where no ordinary player could have done so and he was clearly the architect of victory."

Berry named the "lion-hearted" Johnny Ball as the Wanderers' best player and reckoned things might have turned out differently had Ridding switched Ball and Doug Holden to the left flank to help counter the threat of Matthews and Taylor.

Bolton skipper Moir pithily summed things up at the Café Royal banquet that evening. "We lost because the game was five minutes too long," he said. "Every man in the side ran himself into the ground."

Tommy Banks had been forced to sit in the stand with other family members, including his mother, to watch brother Ralph struggle against a rampant Matthews. Meanwhile Roy was sitting on the touchline with the other reserves glumly witnessing his team mates get carved up.

Reflecting on the match years later, he said: "I felt happy when things were going all right but, when I could see the lads struggling, it was agony. I was sitting there unable to do a thing about it."

Whether or not he could have made a difference, Roy was certainly hoping that he'd soon be back in the side. It's perhaps as well he could not know that two more seasons would pass before his name reappeared on Bolton's first-team sheet.

4

"GOT WED"

If things were not going exactly to plan on the pitch, off it Roy was getting important help to adjust to life in his new surroundings. Although he was no longer the bemused country boy who had first come to Bolton in 1948, especially after those two character-building years in the army, his permanent arrival in the town was still a great culture shock. "I didn't think I would ever settle in Bolton," he admitted.

As well as confronting the obvious differences of living in a large industrial town as opposed to a small village, Roy had to deal with a more exotic lifestyle switch. Put simply, he'd become part of the Bolton entertainment scene rather earlier than expected.

When Roy had travelled up to Bolton from Catshill to play as a young amateur he stayed Friday nights at a large three-storey house in Chadwick Street, off Bromwich Street, run by a Mr and Mrs Rollinson. In those brief weekly visits, the digs had not had much impact on the young Midlander but now he was staying there permanently, he'd begun to notice that his fellow lodgers were a good deal more extraordinary than your average Boltonian. In fact he was sharing a home with an ever-changing assortment of jugglers, comedians, crooners, dancing girls and sword swallowers – unsurprisingly as Mr and Mrs Rollinson ran showbiz digs.

At the time Bolton was home to three theatres, all now footnotes in the town's history, but in 1952 crucial parts of the local entertainment scene. There was the Hippodrome in Deansgate which had its own repertory company, and the Theatre Royal in Churchgate which was where the big bands played. Also in Churchgate was the town's own palace of varieties, The Grand, where audiences would thrill to the top acts of the time, including comedians George Formby and Frank Randle backed up by singing stars of the calibre of Donald Peers and Leslie "Hutch" Hutchinson. And quite a few of these big names stayed at the digs in Chadwick Street.

Roy remembered one particular star who made Mr and Mrs Rollinson's his temporary home. "Max Bygraves stayed there," he said with a chuckle. "He was a bit of a lad was Max. I remember him bringing girls back to the digs. I don't think they were his sisters either." Coincidentally, in Max's later years as a resident of Queensland in Australia, the singer was occasionally ferried around by Roy's son Russell who runs a limousine service in the town of Gold Coast.

Luckily Roy had valuable help in staying grounded among the showbiz folk because just a month after arriving for his second stint at the digs in Bolton, the young footballer met the woman he would marry two years later.

Barbara Hargreaves was the tall, striking looking nineteen-year-old daughter of Elizabeth and Joseph Hargreaves, a farrier who had originally worked with his father Robert in a smithy in Folds Road just outside the centre of Bolton. The family had lived in Hall i'thWood on the edge of town but moved to Hawkshaw near Bury when Barbara was six and then three years later back to Bolton into a council house in Minster Road, Tonge Moor. The move came when Joseph was discharged from the army with phlebitis and, finding fewer horses to shoe due to the introduction of electric milk floats, he took a job as welder at the engineering firm Edbros.

Barbara went to Castle Hill School, which boasted both Nat

Lofthouse and Tommy Lawton as fairly recent pupils. It's perhaps fortunate that Lawton was five years older than Lofty or the sports master Mr Hardy would have had a heck of a job deciding which of these future England centre forwards would wear the number nine shirt in the school football team.

As there were a further seven years between Nat and Barbara, their paths never crossed at school but in later days Barbara remembers that Nat would recall his time as a Castle Hill scholar with affection. "We'd often chat in the tea room at Burnden," she said. "Nat was a great one for going back to the past. He'd say things like, 'They were good old days weren't they, cocker.' Everyone was 'cocker' to him."

Good times or not, schooldays were soon over and at just fourteen it was time to earn a living, in Barbara's case in the book binding department at Tillotson's, the firm which printed the Bolton Evening News in town centre Mealhouse Lane. For twenty-one shillings a week, Barbara would carry out intricate tasks like putting eyelets in paper and repairing broken threads.

"It was when the book had gone through the machine and if anything broke you had to do them by hand," she explained. "You might not think it was very much but it was a very delicate operation and you had to get the thread perfect." When she was not repairing the books, Barbara would occasionally sneak into the printing hall to watch the presses roll. "I used to think it was fascinating, watching all those copies of the paper being printed," she said.

This early fascination for the job did not last and, because employment was easy to find in the late Forties and early Fifties as Britain struggled to get back on its feet after the war, Barbara was soon on the move. Over the next couple of years she took a variety of jobs including shop assistant and office worker before pitching up as a trainee seamstress at the British Tufting Company, a small firm in Bradshaw about a mile from where she lived.

"I was earning about five pounds a week, on piece work making bed linen," she explained. "There were about eight machinists there."

But even though the wages were good Barbara did not particularly enjoy the work and would have been on the hunt for something else – had her mother not discouraged her. "What I really wanted was a good job in an office," she said, "but my mother wanted me to go where I would make money."

Having said that the pay was good, it wasn't quite adequate for the adventure that nineteen-year-old Barbara was planning in March 1952. She explained: "I had already been with two friends to Butlins at Pwlhelli and we enjoyed ourselves so much we got extra jobs so we could go again."

Barbara's extra work was as a part-time waitress at Tognarelli's ice cream parlour in Market Street, Bolton, where the owner would always be seen around the place in a black trilby hat. "He wore it all the time, did Tognarelli," Barbara recalled. "He looked really fierce but he was ever so nice to talk to."

Ironically, taking the weekend job for extra holiday cash meant Barbara would ultimately not be going on that North Wales break with her pals after all. That's because Tognarelli's was a popular haunt for the Bolton Wanderers players, including Roy Hartle, just two months into his professional career.

Jean Edwards, who also met her husband, wing half Bryan, for the first time in the ice cream bar, remembers that the players would pick up their wages on Fridays from Williams Deacons Bank and then saunter across the road into Tognarelli's.

Some, including Roy, would repeat the process on Saturday

morning before the match and that's where Barbara first encountered him. She remembered: "One of my friends, Connie, who worked in Tognarelli's thought Roy fancied her. She said, 'That lad keeps looking over' but he was looking at me."

Recalling the situation with a smile, Roy confirmed that Barbara had got it spot-on. "It was you I fancied not Connie," he said.

Barbara quickly established that the Wanderers players would also spend Saturday evenings at Bolton Palais, the town's main dance hall, which was where she and Roy first got together. It would be splendid to report that it was love at first sight but there was a more down-to-earth reason for Barbara's initial attraction to Roy.

She explained: "I was taller than most of the boys I danced with. So when I saw Roy I thought I'll grab him – so I can wear high heels." The fact that Roy couldn't or wouldn't dance didn't put Barbara off either.

So now they were a couple but, unlike the young women who flock around today's top players, Barbara's reaction to Roy's status was distinctly low-key.

"I wasn't excited at all when I found out he was a footballer," she said. "I didn't even know that footballers were supposed to be exciting. To me it was just that he played football. It didn't ring any bells or anything. I don't think it would do generally in those days. I mean, they're like superstars now but Roy wasn't a superstar when I met him."

Nevertheless there were one or two benefits to stepping out with a footballer. Free tickets to the Capitol and Odeon cinemas for one. Trips to the Theatre Royal and Grand to watch the stars Roy had breakfasted with at Mr and Mrs Rollinson's for another. And then there was eating out – a novel experience for Barbara.

"I thought it was wonderful because I'd never been out for a meal before," she said. "We'd go to the UCP, the Capitol Café and the Odeon café. And eventually we upgraded to the Commercial Hotel." Anyone born in Bolton during the post-war baby boom or before, will recognise the height of luxury implicit in that Commercial upgrade!

Another new experience for Barbara was visiting Burnden Park. Nine months after she'd first spotted Roy in Tognarelli's, she was there on New Year's Day 1953, standing on the terraces with the rest of the fans to see him make his debut against Charlton. And she soon had to learn to accept what the Manchester Road Paddock crowd was saying about her boyfriend. At that first match it wasn't too bad. "I was standing with my Dad," she said, "when they came out on to the pitch and I remember someone shouting, 'Bloody hell, he's a big bugger.' "

However, Barbara quickly had to become accustomed to much more critical stuff, particularly from opposition fans objecting to Roy's already burgeoning reputation as a tough guy full-back.

Something that happened a season or two later in Roy's career summed this up. "One game they played Everton at Bolton and Roy tackled the winger," she said. "The Everton fans didn't like it. So when we went to Everton later in the season, they booed Roy from running on, every time he got the ball, to running off. They never stopped for an hour-and-a-half. I was with some friends, a middle-aged couple, and they were jumping up defending Roy. I was cowering in my seat."

Off the pitch things were happening in a much more orderly fashion. Twelve months on from their first meeting, Roy and Barbara became engaged after the 1953 FA Cup Semi-Final against Everton with Roy calculating that his bonus from the game would go a long way towards the £37 cost of the ring. And, exactly a year after that, they became a married couple.

BARBARA'S DAD, JOSEPH . . . at work as a farrier in Bolton.
(Bolton Evening News)

SPLASH HIT ...
Barbara, aged 17,
at Butlin's, Pwllheli.

JUST MARRIED ...
the happy couople on their
wedding day.
(Bolton Evening News)

PROUD DAD ...
Roy with toddler daughter
Beverley during a 1958 holiday
at Woolacombe, Devon.

"My mother had asked me to give her six months' notice," said Barbara. "But in the end I only gave her four. She had to save up for the wedding."

Roy's only recorded reaction to the big day could be described as somewhat understated. For the 1953-54 season he had a pocket-sized dark blue Football Association diary in which he meticulously recorded who Bolton were playing, his own position and the opponent he faced. These entries include names which were to become very well-known. For instance on September 12th 1953 Roy recorded that the Manchester United left-winger up against him that day in the Reserves was eighteen-year-old David Pegg, the Busby Babe who would go on to win one England cap in 1957 before losing his life at Munich a few months later. Other noted opponents included Colin Grainger, of Sheffield United, who would win seven England caps, Geoff Bent of United, another Munich victim and future Republic of Ireland international Paddy Fagan, who played for Manchester City.

However, it is the entry for March 20th 1954 which really catches the eye. After carefully noting that the first team beat Aston Villa 3-1 and Bolton Reserves had gone down 2-1 to Barnsley, Roy recorded simply, "Day off. Got wed."

If there had been more space for that day's diary entry, Roy would have been able to record that the wedding service was at St Maxentius Church, Bradshaw, during which Barbara was given away by her Dad, Joe. Roy's best man was his brother in law Pat O'Mahoney, the husband of his second youngest sister, Vera. Pat and Vera were among a group of family members who had travelled up from the Midlands the day before but sadly the group did not include either Roy's father or mother, who were both unwell.

The service, conducted by the appropriately named Rev E.

Bradshaw Clarke, was followed by a reception at the Co-op Hall on Bridge Street in the centre of Bolton and, although the wedding meal would seem frugal by today's standards, it was a lot more appetising than it would have been a year or two before. This was because finally after nearly eight years of peace, rationing was coming to an end. Sweets and sugar had become freely available the previous month and, although supplies of meat were still officially limited, butchers were less inclined to ask for ration books. There were even reports of shops being unable to get rid of less appetising cuts of meat that the public would have been begging for a couple of years before.

To emphasise the general tenor of those straitened times, Roy and Barbara left the reception in style in a taxi – which dropped them at Moor Lane bus station where they caught a coach to Blackpool. The honeymoon took place at the classier north end of the resort, not quite at The Savoy but next to it at the Devon Hotel, a small guest house.

"There were all these old dears there," said Barbara. "I don't know whether they were residents, and they were all looking at us from behind their magazines. We were the only young couple there."

The honeymoon didn't even last a week either - just four rainy, windy March days as Roy had to back in training for Saturday's reserve match against Sheffield United. According to the diary, it finished 1-1, ("Capt, full-back, Grainger").

∾ ∾ ∾

Marriage meant a move across town, away from the hoofers, jugglers and sword swallowers at the showbiz digs in Chadwick Street. The newly-wedded couple's destination was a Wanderers club house in Woodgate Street, Great Lever, for which they paid seventeen shillings and sixpence a week rent – with a colony of cockroaches thrown in for nothing.

"We didn't know we'd got them until we moved in," explained Barbara. "The house was fine, apart from these things which only came out at night. We'd go out and come home to find them all running about. Big ones, little ones, brown ones, black ones. It wasn't as though the house was dirty either. I even used to mop the step and the flags outside. Everybody did in those days."

Indeed they did and, if you'd had to design a Northern working class thoroughfare from scratch, you would have struggled to come up with something more typical than Woodgate Street and, parallel to it Eustace Street, where I was approaching my first birthday at number 36. These streets had dark red Accrington brick terraced houses, uneven grey pavements and cobbled roadways which sloped steeply down to the enormous Beehive Mill looming above everything around it like a fortress. All that was missing were the dreamy strains of Dvorak's New World Symphony – otherwise known as that theme from the Hovis advert.

In reality there was nothing remotely romantic about either the streets or the cotton spinning mill where my Dad had begun his working career aged fourteen in the mid-1930s. As he lived in Eustace Street, school to the Beehive was a natural progression. His days at St Simon and St Jude C of E Juniors, where he played for the town's schoolboy football team whose other members included Tommy Lawton, were distant memories as Dad became a little piecer at the mill. The little piecer was the one who tied up broken threads as the spinning mules trundled backwards and forwards winding the cotton on to hundreds of spindles. Dad used to reckon he'd do this while the machines were moving in and out which always sounded unlikely to me but others who did the same job swear it was true. If so, it wasn't so much a case of health and safety gone mad as health and safety just gone.

For Roy work too was a few minutes away from his new home. It involved a brisk walk past the Beehive along Crescent Road and a right turn into Weston Street, down which double-decker buses inexplicably but regularly travelled and invariably became wedged under the low rail bridge.

Ten minutes after leaving home, Roy would be at Burnden Park. One advantage of living locally was that he could get to the ground early and have a choice of training kit, which turned out to be important. "Sometimes they didn't all get washed," he said.

For Barbara the working day was considerably more of a challenge. She explained: "Roy was OK as he could walk to the ground but I used to have to catch two buses to work in Bradshaw. They were long days because I'd have to get up at half-past six and it was after six when I was getting home. It was daft really. I should have changed my job."

What made things doubly galling was what often greeted her when she arrived home. Roy would be waiting for his tea, sometimes alone, often with team mates who had spent all afternoon on the golf course, in the snooker hall or at the races.

Roy later admitted, somewhat shamefacedly, that perhaps he should have cooked the evening meal but defends the status quo at that time by claiming: "I didn't know how to." Typically, even from such a great distance in time, Barbara wouldn't let him get away with that. "I didn't know how to either," she countered. "I wasn't brilliant at cooking when we got married. Then I'd come home and they'd be sat waiting for me. They were like playboys. Training two hours a day and then they were off enjoying themselves somewhere."

And expecting their tea on the table when they got home.

Roy's rather half-hearted defence of the Bolton Rat Pack that, "Well, you had to enjoy yourself," only put him further on the back foot in this particular argument, which was decisively ended with Barbara's assertion that: "Footballers want to be married – but they want to be single as well." It's a comment that might resonate with today's grass widows – although it's unlikely they'll be seeing things from the perspective of having travelled home from work on two buses to a two-up two-down rented terraced house with their husband's fans for neighbours.

However, to balance this impression of a devil-may-care sportsman who announces his marriage in two terse words and spends his leisure time loafing at the racetrack or stuck in a sand bunker, it's worth pausing to look at a touching letter Roy sent two years after he and Barbara were married. Dated May 15th 1956, it's written on five sheets of yellow headed notepaper from the Grand Hotel Terminus in Bergen, where the Wanderers were in the middle of a four-match end-of-season tour of Norway. It is a fascinating snapshot of Roy's life and feelings at the time.

Some of the more mundane stuff could have been written on Twitter or Facebook by today's professionals. There are bits about the incessant rainy weather, "I will never call Bolton again," and the lack of anything to do "about the only place I have been yet is the pictures, there is nothing else," plus something that would be totally outside modern players' experience - having to count the pennies. "I don't think I will be buying you anything," he writes "as most things are dear. I was looking at some blouses today and they were £3. I don't think anybody's bought much."

Yet when Roy talks about his relationship with his wife of two years, the letter becomes heart-warming. "The best day's work I ever did was when I first met you," he writes. "I can honestly say I will love and cherish you for the rest of my life. Dearest Babs I keep thinking there is only another three nights and then I shall be with you again. That's what I am longing for more than anything else in the world."

It's not all hearts and flowers though as Roy reveals a degree of vulnerability, mixed in with more than a hint of jealousy. "Have you been looking at any other chaps?" he asks. "I hope you have enough with me; you are always saying you have." The letter ends with a heartfelt plea after the news that he'll be home around 10.30pm on Saturday. "Please try and be there for when I get there. That's the sight I am waiting to see. It would be terrible if I got home to an empty house."

Roy sent other letters home from the Norway tour but this fascinating snippet, showing the softer, more vulnerable side of the First Division's tough guy, is the only one that survives.

Much as he was looking forward to coming home, Roy would not have been able to put his feet up for the rest of the summer or resume his leisure pursuits as, if anything, he worked harder outside the football season than in it. In this early part of his career he had a labouring job with other team mates at the Bolton brewers Magee Marshalls during the close season when the players' pay went down. And then, in the weeks before the new campaign was due to start, the Wanderers would train morning and afternoon. "He used to come home half-dead," Barbara recalled.

"It was worth it though to get fit," said Roy. "And it was great to be training with players like Nat."

Before we leave the domestic scene, there is the matter of Roy's evolving accent to consider. Everyone who knows him will confirm that Roy is a very well-spoken and polite man, something that undoubtedly saved him from being booked more than just once in his whole career. Years later one leading football writer would comment on "the semi-detached urbanity of the voice which has no trace of Bromsgrove ... or Bolton."

But the mystery remains as to exactly when his accent changed from broad Brummie, as his nephew Dennis insists it sounded when they were growing up, to the modulated tones he uses today. Bryan Edwards' wife Jean reckoned that Roy has talked "posh" in all the sixty years she's known him. However, Tommy Banks disagreed, arguing that the plummy voice developed towards the end of his career when Roy became a Conservative councillor in the mid-1960s. Barbara dismissed this interpretation, saying that she never heard Roy speak with a Birmingham accent.

TRAINING DAY ... Roy leads a run behind Burnden Park in the mid-Fifties. Also pictured are (from left) Ralph Gubbins, Nat Lofthouse, John Higgins, Malcolm Barrass and Dennis Stevens. (MercuryPress.co.uk)

"I think it got more refined as he got older," she conceded, "being with the directors. He used to correct me sometimes. I'd say 'spuds' and he'd say *(puts on posh accent)* 'Barbara, you don't call them spuds, they're potatoes.'"

My own conclusion, after weighing up scraps of information I've gathered, is that the accent change probably began during National Service. A combination of leaving home and getting a position of responsibility (PT instructor) was enough to begin the major switch in tone from Jasper Carrott to Jasper Conran.

5

GOLD RESERVES

Roy spent two full seasons in the Reserves after his 1953 Cup Final disappointment; a career setback most certainly, yet they were anything but wilderness years. During that time he met and played alongside most of the £110 team which returned to Wembley in 1958 and came away victorious. Their collaboration culminated in Wanderers winning the Central League title, the first time the club had ever been Reserve team champions and a feat it has repeated only once, in 1994-95.

It's worth looking at the make-up of the 1954-55 Reserves in a bit more detail to pick up clues to how the greater success was achieved three years later. Of the twelve who won the FA Cup in 1958 (and here it would be churlish not to include the two-goal semi-final hero Ralph Gubbins), eight played in that Reserve side with half a dozen clocking up twenty-five appearances or more. The only cup heroes who did not make a Central League appearance that season were established first-teamers Nat Lofthouse, Doug Holden and Bryan Edwards, plus goalkeeper Eddie Hopkinson who was still fourth in the pecking order behind Stan Hanson, Ken Grieves and Arthur Barnard. Of the others, Tommy Banks and Ray Parry played more first team than Reserve matches; Roy was an ever-present, playing forty-two games, closely followed by Reserve team skipper and centre-half John Higgins (40 games); the other four members of the Cup Final team to play significant Central League roles were Derek Hennin (31 games), Gubbins (31), Dennis Stevens (29) and Brian Birch (25).

In addition two former playing stalwarts were in charge of the team. The coach was former Spurs and England forward George Hunt, who'd signed for Bolton in 1938 after a short and relatively unsuccessful spell with Arsenal. Hunt's form had returned with a bang when he arrived at Burnden and he'd scored twenty-three goals in the 1938-39 season before his career, like many others, fell victim to the war, although he made a number of wartime appearances for Bolton. Hunt rejoined Wanderers as a coach in 1948 after a short spell as a player with Sheffield Wednesday.

The Reserve team's trainer was an even more illustrious part of the Burnden story – he'd even lived at the ground! Harry Nuttall's dad Jack had been trainer and groundsman whose home was a cottage stuck on the corner of the railway embankment terrace, and Harry made his debut for the Wanderers in 1921. A right half, he'd played in each of the three Cup Final wins of the 1920s and like George Hunt, won three England caps. He'd become Reserve team trainer in 1935.

Under their guidance the 1954-55 Reserves won twenty-six, drew seven and lost just nine of their games to claim the Central League trophy. Most satisfyingly they achieved a convincing double over another team whose own youth policy was already attracting national attention – Manchester United, with Bolton winning 3-0 at Old Trafford and 3-1 at Burnden. Moreover, the team was allowed to express itself. Of Hunt and Nuttall, Brian Birch, then a sixteen-year-old said: "They didn't really restrict you. They let you play to your own style and strengths. The good players in the team were Dennis Stevens, John Higgins and Roy. Roy was one of the mainstays. He wasn't frightened of anyone."

Birch also recalled that the side had an excellent team spirit; a theme taken up by Roy as well. Describing his two seasons in the

Reserves as among the happiest of his career, Roy said: "That was the start of the '58 side coming through. Six or seven of that side went into the first team over the space of six or twelve months. That was when everybody worked for each other and the atmosphere and the craic in the dressing room was absolutely incredible."

He added: "If someone wasn't doing particularly well the other lads would get round him and pull through. It was a case if X wasn't having a good game then Y and Z would cover for him."

Of course that kind of spirit is not at all unusual in football dressing rooms. What singles this Bolton side out as rather special, however, is that the great spirit of togetherness persisted long after the 1958 squad had broken up. Eleven of its members (Derek Hennin died tragically early, aged fifty-seven, in 1989) continued to have regular social gatherings well after the turn of the century, when most of them were approaching or were over seventy years old. As Roy said in 2002: "We still have the same passion for one another and I think that's incredible. The respect we had for each other has continued to this day."

That season saw Roy score his first goal for the club, a thirty-yard special in an otherwise mediocre 2-0 home win against Aston Villa Reserves. The Central League title was clinched on the final day of April 1955 with a 1-0 win against Preston at Deepdale and the triumph was given added emphasis the following Monday with a similar victory at Molineux over Wolves. A 23rd-minute goal from seventeen-year-old Jack Pollitt gave Wanderers Reserves their ninth away victory of a season in which they had conceded just twenty-eight goals. For good measure Roy completely snuffed out the threat from left-winger Jimmy Mullen, already an established England international and set to become a key force in Wolves' championship-dominating side later in the decade. On the way back home from the

Midlands the team bus stopped in Staffordshire, at the Crown Hotel, Stone, for a celebration meal and drinks, during which the happy young footballers were congratulated on their achievement by club vice-chairman Ted Gerrard.

However, while a good spirit especially among the up-and-coming youngsters is a real bonus, any Reserve team's prime function is to feed promising talent into the first eleven. Birch and Gubbins were handed their first team debuts in 1954-55 and, of the previous season's debutants, Stevens and Hennin were each given significant roles with the seniors. The skipper, John Higgins, also made the first team for a couple of matches. The only regular player in that Reserve side not to make it into the first team that season was Roy Hartle. But he would not have long to wait.

⁂

Roy made his second first-team debut, if you can call it that, after two games of the following season in a 1-0 defeat at Cardiff. From that day, August 31st 1955, until March 16th 1966 when he pulled on a Bolton first team shirt for the final time, Roy missed just twenty league and cup games. The match also marked the real start of the fearsome and feared Hartle-Banks combination which lasted until the beginning of the 1960-61 season. But, while Roy was absent for just twelve games in that time, Tommy struggled with a series of injuries and missed the equivalent of a season-and-a-half (sixty-five games). "I had a lot of trouble with my legs," he explained, "or we'd have played a lot more together." Tommy also blames injuries for shortening his promising international career.

In popular folklore Hartle and Banks can hardly be separated - uncompromising gravel rash merchants who'd dump you on the track around Burnden Park as soon as look at you. Each liked to get a tackle in early before their opponent had settled on the ball. And both viewed most wingers as, in Tommy's evocative phrase, "yellow bellies". There were honourable exceptions to this tag. For instance neither full-back would hear a word against the great Tom Finney's skill, courage or commitment. And both admired the Leicester and West Brom winger Derek Hogg, who refused to be intimidated by Roy. Tommy explained: "Roy clattered him a few times but he used to get up and have a do back. He wasn't scared at all - but most wingers were. When they came to Burnden they were frightened to death."

However, there were differences between the two full-backs on the pitch, the most obvious being their attitude to the halfway line. For Roy, in this early part of his career it was generally an invisible barrier not to be crossed. He was hardly unique in this for, as we'll see in a subsequent chapter, the idea of the overlapping full-back was generally unheard of. Yet for Haydn Berry this was evidently a source of frustration as early on in Roy's career he saw qualities which he thought elevated the right back above the level of a mere big-boot merchant. Berry remembers a walk back up Manchester Road into town early in Roy's career with the young full-back listening "without a murmur of impatience or protest" while the football journalist expounded on "soccer finesse." It presents new facets to the impression that many people may have of Roy.

"My point," wrote Berry years later in Roy's testimonial brochure, "was that Roy, by nature a robust defender, could add to his game a little more polish and style without sacrificing its effectiveness and with a better chance of catching the eye of the 'Big Wigs' some day!

"We knew well enough he would never be made into a Warney

Creswell or Alf Ramsey but I could, and did, mention internationals of the past who started out in rough, tough style and added a bit of lustre later with great success, Stan Cullis for one.

"Roy listened courteously and though to the end of his playing career he remained above all, a hard-hitting full back, he did develop constructive facets including the push clearance to a colleague in place of the big boot upfield and the right wing overlap with the powerful cross and big shot."

Tommy on the other hand showed he was more than a kick-and-rush merchant right from the beginning of his career. "George Taylor used to play hell with me for going over the half-way line," he remembers, crediting his great friend, Bryan Edwards with granting him the chance of having freedom to roam. "I played with a wing-half, Bryan, who loved defending. He used to have stitches in his eyebrows every week."

In contrast Roy played behind more attack-minded players so the options for getting forward were more limited. At the beginning of his career the right half was Johnny Wheeler and later Hennin, both of whom needed no encouragement to support the forwards.

What sort of team had Roy stepped back into? According to established star Doug Holden, it was one which was tailor-made to suit the new twenty-three-year-old right back. Holden, one of Bolton's most skilful players, said: "Bolton were a tough old Lancashire team built on a certain tradition. With players like Roy at the back we were very strong defensively and used to kick the hell out of opponents. Players would tackle through the back of other players. It was completely different then; now you daren't breathe on them."

The emphasis on toughness extended to training sessions as well. Holden explained: "Even in practice games you could get injured the way we trained. We'd play six against six and kick the hell out of each other." So Bolton didn't only have tough defenders - just as importantly, the attackers weren't soft either.

Training, when it didn't consist of wearing out the gravel around the pitch, took place on a cinder patch at the back of the Burnden Stand. "You couldn't turn a horse round on there," said Tommy Banks. "There was just one set of posts. It was a laugh and a joke." Matters improved dramatically when, in the mid-1950s, training moved across the valley to the new Bromwich Street complex which had two pitches.

Allied to this robust approach, the other thread which ran through Bolton's style of play was the almost total reliance on its talisman. Put simply, the tactic was to get the ball to Nat as quickly as possible. Even when he was at the end of his career and ravaged by injuries, Lofthouse was still telling young players like Francis Lee to hit him early. Lee explained: "Nat said to me, 'When you get the ball, cocker, I want you to cross it somewhere in between the six-yard line and the penalty spot and make their keeper come for it and I'll do the rest.' He used to love the keeper coming out because he'd go in and hit him. And then they'd be watching for him after that."

However, Tommy Banks thinks there was more than that to the team and they sold themselves short by concentrating on getting the ball up to Lofty at all costs. He said: "It wasn't right on the fella and on us because we had two good inside forwards. Ray (Parry) and Dennis (Stevens) never stopped running. Dougie (Holden) was a good footballer too. It helped George Taylor when we got Bromwich Street too. He'd lots of good ideas."

Despite defeat against Cardiff in the third match of the 1955-56 season, Roy kept John Ball in the reserves for the next match, a 4-1 home win against Arsenal, in which both he and Banky contributed to the team's general improvement with a number of constructive touches. Roy was back to stay and thereafter would not be dropped until he was in his thirty-fifth year.

6

ELEVEN TENNERS

The most celebrated team of local lads who gathered together to snatch the big prize away from a bunch of giants is not the Bolton Wanderers side of 1958, although they were famously all-English and assembled for the grand cost of a £10 signing on fee each. Even the most die-hard Trotters fan should not begrudge Celtic's 1967 Lisbon Lions that particular title. Jock Stein built a unit comprising of eleven men born within thirty miles of Glasgow and who beat the giants of Inter-Milan 2-1 in the European Cup Final after the Italians had gone 1-0 up very early on and then retreated into a characteristic defensive formation inviting the Scots to break them down.

Nevertheless Bill Ridding and George Taylor's achievement in bringing through the nucleus of the 1954-55 Central League Champions and moulding them in with more established stars cannot be over-stated. Even if they weren't all born within thirty miles of Ye Old Pastie Shoppe, they were northern and Midlands lads from England's industrial heartlands. Indeed the southern softy in the team, born nearer London than any of them, was Roy Hartle! Furthermore the club had not dipped into the transfer market since 1952 when it paid £27,000 for Harold Hassall, who had to retire two seasons later due to serious injury.

Yet the image of the plucky £110 team who triumphed against the odds is, I believe, misleading. It makes Bolton appear like a bunch of no-hopers who got lucky when they came up against a hastily cobbled-together post-Munich disaster Manchester United team in the 1958 Cup Final. It's true that just over a fortnight before the air crash which claimed the lives of eight players, United had thrashed Bolton 7-2 in January at Old Trafford with the Wanderers fielding ten of the eleven men who would play at Wembley (Holden was injured). But that doesn't quite tell the whole story.

For instance, if Roy's second 'debut' in 1955 is taken as a starting point, of the six league matches played against United up to the 1958 Final, Bolton won twice as many as they lost. Furthermore Wanderers' four victories in this sequence include a 4-0 pummelling of United in front of 48,000 at Burnden in September 1957. Going back a little further, the title winning Reserve side of 1954-55 did the double over the Reds. And in November 1955 United, then league leaders, were beaten 3-1 at Burnden, fielding a team which contained Duncan Edwards, Eddie Colman, Roger Byrne, David Pegg, Mark Jones and Tommy Taylor.

On March 25th 1957, Old Trafford's floodlights were officially opened before Bolton, in an all-white strip, proceeded to illuminate the evening even further with a scintillating 2-0 win against the league champions and FA Cup finalists. So, while it can't be denied that Busby's Babes were a great side, it's clear that Bolton were more than capable of beating them on the day. Would they have overcome a full-strength United, with Edwards, Taylor, Byrne et al, at Wembley in 1958? Of course no-one will ever know but the previous results suggest that at the very least Bolton would have gone into that game with no signs of an inferiority complex.

As it was they approached the match with a team that had finished ninth in Division One the previous season and would claim fourth spot in 1958-59. Five of that 1958 team were already or would very soon become England internationals (Lofthouse, Hopkinson,

Banks, Parry and Holden) and two more (Hartle and Stevens) would represent The Football League. Whatever Bolton were, it was not no-hopers.

Having said all that, the league campaign up to the start of the Cup run had hardly been outstanding – and wasn't about to get much better. At the beginning of the season hopes were high that the previous campaign's ninth place finish would be bettered, especially as many members of that title-winning Central League side were now firmly established in the first team. But from mid-December to February 18th the Wanderers played eight matches in which they won only once and were beaten five times, including by United who took spectacular revenge for that earlier 4-0 defeat with the 7-2 thrashing of Bolton at Old Trafford, an outstanding Bobby Charlton and Dennis Viollet both grabbing hat-tricks.

So the Cup victories over Preston, York and Stoke were welcome distractions during this otherwise barren period. The Third Round result, 3-0 at Deepdale with two goals from Parry and another from Stevens, was one of the club's best FA Cup performances in a long while and looked especially impressive as Preston were flying high and would finish as First Division runners-up at the end of the season. It was a particularly satisfying afternoon for Tommy Banks and Bryan Edwards who, working in tandem, managed to subdue the great Tom Finney, playing on the right wing. Finney, in his thirty-sixth year, was still a force in English football and in Roy's words "simply the best player I ever came up against." Indeed that day, he was forced by the implacable Banks and Edwards to switch wings where Roy and Hennin proved equally as unyielding.

Lowly York gave Bolton far more trouble in the Fourth Round, holding Wanderers to a goal-less draw at Bootham Crescent before goals from Birch and Terry Allcock (2) ensured the replay ended 3-0.

Stoke, who had already beaten the holders Aston Villa, became the first team in the cup run to score past Eddie Hopkinson and it took a penalty from wing-half Bobby Cairns for that to happen. A memorable feature of the Fifth Round match was Roy's forward charge through a Burnden quagmire at the end of which the Stoke goalkeeper Wilf Hall tipped the full-back's thunderous shot on to the bar – only to see it rebound straight to Parry who stuck it in to complete the scoring in a 3-1 home victory. Lofthouse and Stevens had scored the other goals. However, Bolton's reward for their FA Cup industry was a dubious one – a Sixth Round home tie against arguably the country's top club, the other Wanderers.

It's perhaps difficult to imagine now but the English team most sides least enjoyed playing against in the 1950s was Wolves. Busby's United may have been more admired for their easy-on-the-eye passing style but Stan Cullis's Black Country boys were the ones most teams did not fancy meeting. They were generally faster and a lot fitter than their opponents. And their direct style of play, some called it kick-and-rush, made Bolton look like the Barcelona of today. OK, perhaps not *quite* that but the Wolves style certainly beat any direct kind of play Bolton could dish up. Wolves' particular effectiveness at this form of football was reflected in the league positions. While Bolton were becalmed below mid-table, Wolves were running away with a league they would eventually win by five points in front of Preston (when it was still two points for a win) who, in turn, finished eight points ahead of Spurs in third place. It would be the first of consecutive league championships for Wolves, who would only miss out on a third title by one point in 1959-60 when they won the FA Cup.

This was the fitting backdrop to what many have described as one of the greatest games ever seen at Burnden Park. The Bolton Evening News set the scene in a Cup tie special edition, explaining how Burnden "has emerged from a nightmare week of snow, ice and thaw to become a fit and proper place for the 'Little Wembley' battle. It will take the best Bolton can produce to beat the Midlands' idols."

Most of the 56,303 people who crowded into Burnden on March 1st 1958 could hardly have disagreed with the second sentiment. These would definitely have included the 15,000 fans who had travelled up from Wolverhampton which even dwarfed the considerable invasion by the Stoke supporters in the previous round. However, the notion of the Bolton pitch playing like Wembley needs considerable imagination-stretching as the surface that day soon turned into the mud-heap it had become in the previous round. Tommy Banks typically and memorably described the conditions as "up to the neck," and getting worse.

Against any other side this would have been a colossal advantage to Bolton, who fielded the eleven who would play at Wembley two months later. As it was, they were up against perhaps the one side who would revel in the muddy conditions more than them. The terrible pitch was tailor-made for Wolves with their uncompromising defence, led by England veteran Billy Wright and the tough but skilful wing-halves, Eddie Clamp and young Ron Flowers who would sweep passes out to wingers Jimmy Mullen and Norman Deeley at the earliest opportunity. It would then be a short instant before the ball would arrive in the opposition penalty box to allow inside forwards Bobby Mason and Peter Broadbent and centre forward Jimmy Murray to do their work.

Bolton must therefore take a fair bit of credit for grabbing the lead in the twenty-seventh minute. Birch's sharp cross from the corner of the penalty area found Stevens in an unusual amount of space for a Wolves goalmouth and he poked the ball in from six yards. The lead lasted just two minutes when Wolves equalised through Mason. Eleven minutes after half-time Bolton regained the lead with Parry's skilful free kick after the Wolves' goalkeeper Malcolm Finlayson had handled the ball just outside his area. Apparently Tommy Banks was the architect of the goal. "I said to Ray, 'have a do' because he had a good left foot," he explained, "and he had a do!"

If that seems straightforward then what followed was anything but. The Bolton defence was subjected to the kind of sustained bombardment few of the home spectators had witnessed before – and it was to Bolton's great credit that they stood firm. Roy Hartle alone cleared off the line three times and one of his saving headers flew on to the terraces when it looked easier for him to score an own goal. Thankfully the only thing that ended up in the back of the net was Roy himself. And in the final minutes a mud-bound goalmouth scramble saw Roy and the other defenders repeatedly throw themselves in the way of Wolves forwards' goal-bound attempts.

What had made matters even more precarious for the Wanderers in those final desperate minutes was a series of unsettling injuries. Ray Parry was carried off with concussion eight minutes from time after crashing into Finlayson and was too groggy to celebrate or even appreciate the fact that he'd ended up scoring the winner when the final whistle went. However, what hardly anyone knew was that right half Hennin had pulled a muscle in his leg as early as the fifth minute of the match and bravely played on with the handicap. In the all-for-one one-for-all spirit of that team of firm friends, Stevens dropped back increasingly into the right half position as the second half wore on.

Then there was the problem of Eddie Hopkinson, the final barrier against the relentless bombardment. Gordon Taylor, in the crowd that day as a wide-eyed passionate thirteen-year-old fan of the club he was later to play for with distinction, said: "Eddie Hopkinson told me he'd been banged on the head by Eddie Clamp which had given him double vision. Jimmy Murray was bearing down on him and he hit this shot. Hoppy said, 'I could see these two balls coming at me' and I said 'What did you do, Eddie?' He replied, 'I pushed them both round the post.' "

The fact that the tale has been repeated – and maybe a little embellished – many times since that day doesn't alter the fact that Hopkinson was struggling, increasingly so as the game wore on. As well as the head injury, the constant second half bombardment took its toll on the goalkeeper's stamina. Tommy Banks remembered: "Hoppy were more tired than us. In fact, Roy and I finished up taking the goal kicks."

Unsurprisingly Roy has strong and positive memories of the match. "We took all they could throw at us," he said. "It was an absolutely wonderful game. Wolves were a very, very good side." His full-back partner was in full agreement about the standard of opposition. "Wolves always had a good team," said Tommy. "They ran us to death."

Despite his considerable disappointment, the Wolves and England skipper Billy Wright sportingly went into the Bolton changing room after the match to congratulate the victorious Wanderers players.

The last word on the day goes to Haydn Berry who wrote: "A stirring match if ever there was one; many say the most exciting football match they can recall attending. From Lofthouse downwards they were magnificent in their spirit. No bigger ordeal lies ahead …

They have come through their Cup crisis at the gateway to Wembley and can go forward without fear to the end of this journey."

Bolton weren't quite yet in the shadow of those Twin Towers, however. On the same afternoon, the Second Division pace-setters Blackburn Rovers had also chalked up a 2-1 Sixth Round win, against fellow second tier club Liverpool and as a reward were handed a Semi-Final tie against their near, if not particularly dear, neighbours a dozen miles down the road.

Bolton might have really fancied their chances against a team who had been in the Second Division for a decade had it not been for two factors. Firstly, Blackburn were on the rise. Up-and-coming young stars like Bryan Douglas, Ronnie Clayton, Roy Vernon and Peter Dobing were about to help ensure that promotion near-misses in the previous two seasons would not happen a third time. The second problem was Nat Lofthouse's damaged collar bone. The injury, sustained in a 4-1 away defeat against Spurs eleven days after the epic match against Wolves, was serious enough to warrant an operation and would keep Bolton's talisman out of action for six matches and even threatened his presence in the crowd at the semi. Lofty's absence wouldn't have been such a problem had Bolton not sold their reserve striker just before the March transfer deadline. Terry Allcock, who'd scored two goals to help beat York 3-0 earlier in the campaign, was offloaded to Norwich City where he rapidly became a favourite, helping the Canaries to an FA Cup Semi-Final the following season, and then a legend, ending up as Norwich's second-highest goal scorer of all time.

The man chosen by Bill Ridding to stand in for Lofty was Ralph Gubbins, hardly a tyro as he'd played nearly ninety league and cup games for Bolton up to that point, scoring a dozen times. But Gubbins had appeared in most of those games as a left-winger with the occasional outing at inside-left and, though the goal tally was respectable for someone in those positions, it was hardly in the Lofthouse class; no shame there as few, if any, approached Nat's standard. But neither did it compare with Allcock's record. In the sporadic appearances he'd managed over five seasons, Allcock had averaged a goal every three games.

So it was announced just the day before the match that, after one game back in the first team, a 1-0 defeat by Sheffield Wednesday at Hillsbrough, Ralph Gubbins would become the fifteenth Wanderers player in the Cup run that season, lining up with his team-mates in their new red second kit to take on Blackburn at Maine Road on March 22nd in front of 74,800 spectators. (The other two who had taken part in the cup run were Graham Stanley and Geoff Cunliffe. Both had played in the Fourth Round games against York).

As the First Division side, Bolton went into the match as firm favourites and Roy remembered: "After the titanic effort to beat Wolves I think we were convinced our name was on the Cup."

It's odd that the only game in the march to Wembley that Barbara Hartle has clear memories of is that Semi-Final and then only because of the weather. "It was pouring down," she remembered, "and they gave us seats right on the front row." She also recalls who was the star of the day. "It was Gubby who got us through," she said. "He stood in for Nat and was man of the match that day."

No Bolton fan would surely begrudge Ralph Gubbins that title. After Dobing had scored with a header just inside the post past Tommy Banks from a corner by Ally McLeod, Bolton's stand-in striker had his magic minute. Blackburn had turned up the pressure after their goal and so Bolton's reply was very much against the run of play. In the

38th minute, with Rovers claiming offside, Gubbins calmly slotted the ball past the Blackburn keeper with his left foot from twelve yards. And almost straight from the re-start, a free kick from Tommy Banks found Gubbins on his own in the penalty area and from six yards out the stand-in striker made no mistake. Much as in the Wolves match, Bolton were on the back foot for a lot of the second half as Blackburn pressed for the equaliser. But Eddie Hopkinson, back from injury, was equal to everything thrown at him and helped by the defence who dug in, Bolton booked a Wembley Cup Final date for the second time in five years. After the final whistle Nat raced onto the pitch to embrace stand-in skipper John Higgins who later admitted: "That was our worst match of the season." Higgins further revealed that the whole team had been afflicted by nerves and young Brian Birch was in such a state that, "I practically had to help him on to the field."

After the win, though, nobody seemed to mind much about nerves or under-par displays and the players partied at Bolton's Pack Horse Hotel, where Nat toasted Ralph in champagne and admitted: "I couldn't have done better myself."

Haydn Berry too could not fail to be impressed, writing: "He wasn't everyone's choice, even as the stop-gap, but Gubbins the slender winger turned centre-forward kept a cool head twice during fleeting moments of indecision by the Rovers defenders and made neat little goals out of both situations."

And Roy added his own generous tribute to Wanderers' two-goal hero. "Thankfully Ralph came up with the goods when they were needed with two quick goals which were enough to see us through to the Final."

However, the joy of reaching the Cup Final would soon be tempered by the identity of the team they'd have to face on May 3rd. For, after a 2-2 draw at Villa Park that afternoon, Manchester United travelled to Highbury the following Wednesday and overcame Fulham 5-3 in the replay.

After the Munich air crash, in which the United manager Matt Busby was badly injured, his assistant Jimmy Murphy had taken charge. United had been given the option of dropping out of the FA Cup but Murphy managed to cobble together a side of youngsters and hasty signings, including Ernie Taylor who had actually turned out for Blackpool in earlier rounds but was given special dispensation to play for another club in the Cup. Although United's league form collapsed – they won just one of the remaining league matches up to the end of the season – the FA Cup proved a different story. When the crash happened United were already through to the Fifth Round after wins over Workington and Ipswich. Thirteen days after the disaster they beat Sheffield Wednesday 3-0 in a highly emotionally charged atmosphere and got through the Sixth Round after a replay against West Brom followed by the two-match Semi against Fulham.

So, for the second time in five years Bolton were in a Final that only their own supporters wanted them to win, while their opponents wallowed in a sea of goodwill. This emotion had been fairly simple for Bolton players and supporters to brush aside in 1953. Although he was already an iconic figure in English football, Stan Matthews had no divine right to an FA Cup winner's medal and nor would he argue that he had. This was illustrated by the effort he had to put into the 1953 Final's later stages to earn that gong.

In 1958, however, the emotion was harder to deal with as there were a number of close ties between the old Manchester United side and Bolton. Roy and Banky had remained close friends with Tommy Taylor since their army days. Lofthouse played in a number of international matches alongside Roger Byrne and Duncan Edwards and had then seen Taylor replace him as England centre-forward. He paid Taylor the ultimate accolade, saying: "If he hadn't died in the Munich air crash he would have become the greatest centre-forward of them all." Hopkinson had been in goal during the United trio's final three England matches, the last against France at the end of November 1957. And Roy remembers some testing encounters with left-winger David Pegg. "He was such a good player," he said, "mind you they all were. Tommy Taylor was unbelievable, absolutely unbelievable."

There were social ties too. Bolton players including Roy, Tommy and Bryan Edwards would often take their wives on a Saturday night out to the Cromford Club at the bottom of Market Street in Manchester. The club was owned by one of the city's characters, Paddy McGrath, a close friend of Matt Busby which made the Cromford a natural haunt for the United squad.

"A lot of United players used to go there," said Jean Edwards. "And the Bolton lads were friendly with them."

Then there was the regular socialising when the game was over. Barbara explained: "After the match we'd all go into the tea room at Burnden. It was just really a kind of wooden hut about half the size of our living room. There'd be a crate of beer for the men and sherry for the wives. The place would be full of smoke as everyone either smoked cigarettes or pipes." Barbara remembers that after one match at Burnden, the United skipper Roger Byrne told her the name of his pipe tobacco and, unsurprisingly, it's a name that has stuck in her memory. "He told me it was called Baby's Bottom. I've never forgotten that."

She clearly remembered the day of the crash. "We heard about it on the television and I can remember Roy telling me to shut up, which wasn't like him at all. He was so upset and shocked. We knew them all."

However, the most poignant connection between the pre-Munich Manchester United and Bolton Wanderers was a family one. Dennis Stevens and Duncan Edwards were cousins brought up in the Birmingham suburb of Dudley and both had played for the area's schoolboy side at the same time. The highly-rated Edwards was just twelve when he got into the team, some three years younger than his cousin Dennis.

Before United were to be faced there was a season to finish – and it was not a particularly distinguished end to the campaign. Bolton played eight league games and only won one, a 4-0 thrashing of Aston Villa in which the stand-in centre forward Hennin grabbed a hat-trick. Ridding had switched Gubbins to inside left for that game but he was back at centre forward after Hennin was injured in his next game as striker, a 2-0 defeat by Manchester City. Two matches later and Lofthouse returned for the final three games of the season although they drew one and lost the other two, including a 4-0 Burnden beating by Preston, which featured a Finney penalty given after Roy had barged the Preston skipper in the back.

The only two goals Bolton managed in those three final matches were scored by the returning skipper. I was about to write "so his Cup Final place was secure," but really there was never any doubt that, if fit, Lofthouse would play at Wembley. Yet, how could you possibly leave out the man who scored the two goals that got Bolton into the Final? Maybe someone else would make way for Gubbins. But of the other four forwards Parry and Stevens had scored nearly as many as the skipper in league and Cup (Stevens, 15, Parry, 18 and Lofthouse 20) and both had shown impressive form until the late season league dip during which Parry missed four games. Holden too would be almost impossible leave out. He was the only player other than Lofthouse who had Wembley Cup Final experience and at twenty-seven, he was at his peak and considered by many to be one of Bolton's finest post-war players, a fact soon to be recognised by England manager Walter Winterbottom who gave him five international starts during 1959. The other factor in Holden's favour was the number of dangerous crosses he supplied for Lofthouse to take advantage of.

The same thing could also be said for the right-winger Brian Birch who liked to get the ball across as early as he could so Lofthouse could steal a march on the opposing centre-half. However, it looked as if Birch was the most vulnerable to being dropped, if only because he was not part of the squad during the week.

He explained: "I was still in the RAF doing my National Service at the time of the Final but I'd played in every round. I had to do my own training at the airfield and there was some doubt in my mind whether I would play after Ralph scored two in the semi-final. But, to be fair, Bolton never gave me the impression that I wouldn't be playing."

Birch's National Service duties meant he missed the club's trip to Blackpool's Norbreck Hydro hotel where the players and management stayed from Tuesday to the Saturday before the Final. The trip which included golf, walking and brine baths was a particular treat for two future Wanderers stalwarts, close pals Syd Farrimond and Freddie Hill, who were both seventeen. There was also ball work at Rossall School, near Blackpool, where the turf was reckoned to be more like Wembley than any in the region.

Birch joined the squad on the Saturday for the season's final game against Burnley, at Turf Moor. It was clear that most of the team had their eyes on the following Saturday and nobody was particularly surprised when Bolton lost 3-1. The only plus came when Hennin returned after a four-match absence and, though he looked rusty, at least his injured leg stood up to the test.

The following Tuesday the Wanderers' Cup Final team went up on the board – and Ralph Gubbins found out he would not be playing at Wembley.

Roy was sympathetic – he'd been in that very position five years earlier. "I felt for Ralph when he wasn't picked, especially as it was like what happened to me in '53," he said. In fact Gubbins, like Roy five years before, had already lost his first team place by the time the Final came round and can hardly have been too surprised when he was left out of the Wembley line-up. And, while sympathising with the semi-final hero, Roy agreed that it was right that Lofthouse should have been picked. "Nat was our best player," he said. "To have gone into the Final without him would have been unthinkable."

However, in the years after 1958, few Bolton supporters forgot the vital contribution made by Ralph Gubbins to the Cup triumph and to many he is regarded as the honorary twelfth member of the winning team. Indeed, a special plate which celebrates the Wanderers' Cup Final victory confirms this as Gubbins' name is placed centrally on the plate with the names of the other players forming a kind of guard of honour. The special regard for the Semi-Final hero is borne out by the many heart-felt tributes when he died in September 2011. On the Bolton fans' website Wanderers Ways you can still see the grateful and affectionate comments of supporters, many of who were not born in 1958. Roy added his own simple tribute. "He was a good friend and a true gentleman."

The day after the team was chosen, the squad had a training session at Bolton School followed by a trip back to Burnden where they were treated to Bill Ridding's magic potion, raw eggs beaten up in sherry. Roy remembers the formula was what the manager, called "special training". "Mind you," added Roy, "we only got it before big Cup matches. Couldn't afford it for league games."

Another dose of magic came when the prolific mind reader Al Koran, due to start a week's booking at the Grand Theatre, ditched his usual practice of placing predictions in envelopes to be opened after the event and came straight out with the forecast that Bolton would win 3-1.

Buoyed by the magical prospect of a two-goal winning margin, Wanderers travelled down to London by coach on Thursday May 1st. Just as in 1953, the squad was staying at the Hendon Hall Hotel, a former Georgian mansion just a couple of miles from Wembley. On arrival in the capital they were taken straight to the House of Commons for a tour followed by a meal as guests of the two Bolton MPs, the Liberal Arthur Holt and Philip Bell QC, who represented Bolton East for the Conservatives. In the evening the Bolton lads watched an England side play the Under 23s at Stamford Bridge.

Most of the squad got their first taste of Wembley the following morning and it was on arrival at the stadium they learned that they had been allocated the north side dressing room used by Blackpool in 1953. Then it was off to a training session at nearby Hendon FC's ground before some of the players took an opportunity to visit Lord's cricket ground and watch the match between MCC and Yorkshire, a moderately low-scoring affair in which Fred Trueman took six wickets for 41 runs.

Meanwhile the wives and girlfriends, due to travel down to London on Friday, were busy too. Some decided that if the men could have their

Cup Final suits from Jacksons the Tailors in Deansgate then they'd have special outfits as well. Jean Edwards explained: "Persianelle fur coats came out around that time and I got one and Barbara got one. When you think of how you dress for football matches these days, well we used to go in high heels and these coats. We were WAGs," she added with a laugh.

Barbara confirmed that they had fur coats but said she and Jean did not wear them for the Final, which was on a hot Spring day. She said: "Before the Final the BBC came and interviewed us and we were walking up and down Newport Street in these Persianelle coats. We thought we were the bee's knees in them. But for the Final I had a light navy suit and then I got a red coat." Predictably, given who Bolton were about to face, Roy was less than pleased. "He said, 'You can't wear that!' " remembered Barbara.

By Friday evening, some players were beginning to feel the strain. And, unlikely as it seems, Nat Lofthouse was one of them. Despite the thirty-one caps he had won for England (there would be two more) and the adoration of the Bolton public, the only actual medal our town's leading legend had picked up during his career was a loser's gong in 1953. And, despite the precedent of Stan Matthews, Nat realised that at the age of thirty-two this was in all likelihood his last opportunity to win a football honour. Eddie Hopkinson, who shared a room with Nat, revealed how anxious his skipper was the night before the final. Nat told him: "We've got to win tomorrow, Hoppy. It could be my last chance to get that medal."

As Saturday dawned, the remainder of the Wanderers playing staff and officials left Burnden on coaches for Manchester to catch the train to London. All bar one that is. Syd Farrimond's 58 bus from near his Hindley home was late which meant he was behind schedule when he caught the 42 from Bolton which went past the ground. And when he got there, the coaches had all gone. The seventeen-year-old left back, yet to make his debut for the first team, was incredulous. "I thought, 'They've left me. What have they left me for'? There used to be a phone box at the corner of the car park so I thought I'll phone for a taxi. I must have had about a fiver on me. Anyway the taxi came and I still remember that the fare was thirty bob (£1.50) to Manchester. And I just made it in time."

In the Midlands meanwhile, the Hartle clan were preparing a mini-invasion of London. Roy's nephew Dennis said: "I didn't go to the Final in 1953 although my Dad (Roy's much older brother Len) did. This time I was determined not to miss out and we hired a twelve-seater mini coach. I don't think any of Roy's brothers went but the sisters and their husbands did."

Roy had ensured that his family was well-supplied with match tickets but not everyone was as fortunate and it was later reported that "the black market in Cup Final tickets reached an enormous peak … open auctions were held along all roads leading to the stadium." A three shillings and sixpence ticket was seen to sell for £9 and stand tickets were going for £20.

Whether they had a ticket or not, at least nobody would go hungry. 15,000 extra sandwiches and 5,000 extra pies had been shipped in to Euston, St Pancras and Marylebone railway stations to feed the 25,000 fans from both clubs arriving there.

If some had been gripped by pre-match nerves, it was a different type of emotion that surfaced as the Bolton boys started their journey to the stadium. Remembering the old friends and rivals who they would never face again, Roy explained that he felt an air of sadness hung over the whole occasion. "There were tears shed on the coach and that included me. It was extremely difficult."

As the two teams lined up alongside each other in the Wembley tunnel, it was time for more traditional doubts and fears to resurface. These days Roy says he can't recall having any pre-match nerves. "I don't know why but I didn't feel like I was under any kind of pressure," he told me. However Tommy Banks remembers that Roy seemed "a bit edgy" a feeling he shared, claims Banky, with Birch and Edwards, although Holden was calmness personified. And, as for Tommy himself, he reckoned, "It was just another match as far as I was concerned."

While a still-convalescing Matt Busby was present at the match, his team were led by Jimmy Murphy who strode out into the bright sunlight ahead of a side which included four Munich survivors and just two players, Bill Foulkes and Bobby Charlton, who had appeared in the Cup Final defeat against Aston Villa twelve months earlier. Their colleague, thirty-seven-year-old inside right Ernie Taylor, was one of three men on the pitch that afternoon who had played in the 1953 Final. The others were Lofthouse and Holden, who took their place in the line as Bill Ridding led out the Wanderers.

Any Bolton butterflies still present during the pre-match presentations to Prince Philip were largely banished when Lofthouse managed to grab his customary early Cup Final goal. Unlike in 1953, when the centre forward netted after 75 seconds, the Bolton fans had to wait until the third minute before they could celebrate. United failed to clear properly from a Holden corner and Edwards picked up the ball twenty yards out before curling a low cross to the far post where the Bolton skipper was waiting, unmarked, to stab it in from six yards.

It looked as if the goalkeeping jitters which had been such a feature of Farm and Hanson's performances five years earlier had resurfaced when Harry Gregg spilled a couple of crosses. But, after making fine saves from Lofthouse, Birch and Holden, United's Northern Irish 'keeper seemed to have settled down. For the Wanderers, Hopkinson had started confidently and then got even better with great back-to-back saves mid-way through the half from Taylor and Charlton. Roy, too, seemed largely untroubled by the player facing him, Colin Webster. And, on the other side of the pitch, Tommy Banks was already starting to lay his claim to be named man of the match with an authoritative and skilful display against Alex Dawson and occasionally Webster when he switched wings. Both Wanderers full backs now agree that their tasks were made considerably easier by the fact that neither opponent was actually a winger. Webster played most of his games as an inside forward and Dawson was an eighteen-year-old centre forward at the start of his career. "I suppose they thought he'd keep me quiet," Tommy told me. "But he didn't. He were only a lad and he weren't a winger."

So, while United had occasionally threatened the Bolton goal with Charlton and Viollet looking lively, the general view was that a determined Bolton were well worth their 1-0 half-time lead. Moreover, the Wanderers started the second half with a real determination to put the match to bed. Almost immediately Roy was in the action with a superb forty-yard ball to Stevens, whose right wing cross was plucked out of the air at a stretch by Gregg. Not long afterwards Lofthouse tricked his way into a shooting position on the edge of the area but his effort flew well over the bar.

The pivotal moment of the match came seven-and-a-half minutes after the interval when Viollet got on the end of a long cross-field ball from Charlton and played it first time into the Bolton penalty area. Roy just about managed to get a touch on the ball but it fell straight to Taylor who threaded it through to the unmarked Charlton. His first-time right foot shot flew past Hopkinson – and cannoned against the post straight back into the relieved Bolton keeper's hands. Trying not to sound like the Wanderers supporter he undoubtedly was, the TV commentator Kenneth Wolstenholme, a Farnworth lad, reckoned that Hoppy was, "As lucky as a man with half a dozen tickets for My Fair Lady after that." He was perhaps even luckier than that as just over two minutes later Bolton went further ahead in famously controversial circumstances.

While the much-discussed second goal of the 1958 FA Cup Final could hardly be described as a thing of beauty, the move that led up to it was a belter. It began when Holden headed a Gregg clearance to Parry near the left touchline. He checked back, away from Foulkes, and returned it to Holden who moved inside before squaring it towards Stevens. Instead of trapping the ball, however, the inside-right stepped over it, allowing Edwards enough time to collect it and spot Holden who was now on the front edge of the box. In the meantime, Stevens had spun away into the inside left position where he was in the clear to receive a clever flick from Holden, who diverted Edwards' pass into his path. Stevens' ferocious left-foot shot was palmed into the air by Gregg and, as the 'keeper turned towards his goal to gather the dropping ball, Lofthouse hurtled in and bundled both ball and man into the net for possibly the most famous shoulder charge of all time. It was an unlovely finish to a terrific move and, with the United defenders displaying bemusement rather than outrage, the referee Jack Sherlock pointed to the centre spot.

However, the United players' attitude soon changed to one of anger when they saw Gregg stretched out in the goal behind his line. This quickly turned to concern as the United backroom staff made frantic efforts to revive the goalkeeper. Just over two minutes after Lofthouse's challenge Gregg was on his feet again, although it would be nearly a further two minutes before the game re-started during which time the United trainer Jack Crompton administered a prolonged dose of smelling salts to the keeper. His recovery can't have been helped by a lusty chorus of "The Happy Wanderer" belted out by the Bolton supporters.

When I discussed the incident with Roy, he gave the ghost of a chuckle at the memory before agreeing it was a foul, adding: "He certainly wouldn't get away with it today would he?" Doug Holden expressed an identical view and even Lofty, who was booed throughout the rest of the second half, has agreed the challenge was questionable. He said: "A foul? Looking back, yes. Today I would probably have been sent off. But in those days you could challenge the keeper. That's what I did. I didn't go in to hurt Gregg. I went for the ball. And that's how the referee saw it. When I looked round he was pointing to the centre circle. Goal. I don't argue with referees." A decade later Nat admitted: "If I'd barged a goalkeeper like that these days I'd probably have been sent off."

For his part, the incident left Gregg sore both literally and metaphorically. Three years later he wrote: "I knew I had taken quite a battering – and the middle of the back isn't recognised as a normal place for a shoulder charge," and went on to say that if he'd had the chance he would have gained his revenge on Nat. However, in later years he mellowed and said of Nat: "There are no bad feelings between us. I respect him enormously."

Among those United defenders who watched anxiously as Gregg lay dazed was right-half Freddie Goodwin. His thoughts about the incident are still clear. Goodwin, who would play a pivotal part in

Roy's life nine years later, told me: "My memories of the 1958 Cup Final are not ones I treasure although it was a great honour to play in the Final. The result was marred by Bolton's second goal when Nat Lofthouse charged our goalkeeper over the line."

Bobby Charlton has always been more sanguine about the matter, probably because the 1958 Final is hardly central to the glittering career he would go on to have. Of much more importance was that, despite what had recently happened to him, he was still playing top-level football.

Haydn Berry's initial reaction was to dismiss the incident. In his match report he states: "Some mild attempt to make capital out of the incident by a small section of the crowd quickly died away for lack of support, especially as Gregg appeared to be unaffected by the fall."

The final word on the matter, as in many things, goes to Barbara Hartle, who briskly pointed out: "Like Nat always said, 'We'd got another goal so we'd still have won.'"

Mr Sherlock's lenient approach to robust challenges persisted throughout the half culminating in an incident in the 85th minute which left Dennis Stevens lying flat out on the turf. Whether by accident or design, the forehead of United's outside-left, Colin Webster appeared to collide with Stevens' face and flatten him. Yet, the ref decided nothing untoward had happened and told the pair to shake hands and get on with the match. Which they did.

In the 90th minute a tidy build-up involving Lofthouse, Parry and Holden ended with Birch just failing to make contact with his left-winger's cute pass but selling a dummy to Gregg in the process. However, the ball was cleared off the line by United left-back Ian Greaves, later to become a Burnden favourite with his Wanderers promotion-winning team of the late Seventies.

The match ended with Lofthouse bursting clear of the United defence, only to be thwarted by the final whistle, whereupon the Bolton skipper embraced his delighted manager who had dashed on to the field.

It hadn't been a particularly great Final, and certainly came nowhere near matching the quality and excitement of the 1953 game, but the consensus was that Bolton had looked sharper, stronger and more determined than United. Haydn Berry summed it up like this: "It was won by the best of all Cup formulas – solid unshakeable defence and scoring opportunism allied to the will to win. Manchester United were ... not as good opposition as expected even after allowing for their hastily-built force and the Wanderers' win was the easiest of the series, apart from the York replay."

Bill Holden, writing in the Daily Mirror, reckoned the match had been dubbed "dreary" only because United had lost. Under the headline "What an insult to Bolton," Holden wrote: "Never has a team played so well for so little acclaim."

Watching the BBC recording today, it's difficult not to conclude that Roy had a quiet match without putting a foot wrong. Looking back on that hot May day across a gap of over fifty years Roy said simply and humbly: "I didn't have a particularly great match but I don't think I let anybody down either." Another Bolton Evening News sports writer, The Pilgrim, disagreed, writing: "Hartle had an excellent game."

However, the columnist reserved his greatest praise for Lofthouse, Hopkinson and Banks, "for as fine a display as one could wish to see." The left-back's man-of-the-match performance certainly justified his inclusion in the England squad for the forthcoming World Cup in Sweden. Of the Cup Final, Tommy said: "I was always confident we'd beat them. In fact I was disappointed we only won 2-0."

For the under-par United, Ernie Taylor proved a shadow of the player who had helped Stan Matthews torment Bolton in the later stages of the 1953 Final. However, one player at the other end of his career had shown flashes of the promise that would turn him into a world superstar. Bobby Charlton, nominally centre forward but already playing in a familiar deeper lying midfield role, displayed touches of the form that would illuminate this same stage in an even bigger match eight years later.

So the Bolton players were well worth the FA Cup and winners' medals handed to them by Prince Philip. And a lap of honour, of course. Except that two of the team, their minds still on friends who had been killed at Munich, would have denied themselves that honour and sloped off back to the changing rooms had it not been for Bolton trainer Bert Sproston.

Roy explained: "Tommy and I stood at the bottom of the steps after collecting our medals and he just said, 'Come on, let's go'. And we would have done too if Bert hadn't caught us. He told us this was probably the most important day of our lives and, if we didn't go round the ground we'd always regret it."

Tommy confirmed the story. He said: "After the game I said to Roy, 'Come on let's go. We don't want all this hurdy-gurdy messing about.' And Bert Sproston said, 'Get round this field. It's a memory you'll never forget. It's history.'"

The story, told many times over since then, is even quoted with approval by the old enemy. On one of the United fans' websites (I go there so you don't have to) there's a particularly thoughtful and well-written article which pays tribute to Nat not long after his death in January 2011. While the article is not all hearts and flowers stuff, especially in relation to the second goal in the 1958 Final, its writer Giles Oakley recognises the special nature of how the Bolton full-backs felt that day. He writes: "Banks and Hartle were both hardened 'old school' dump 'em in the cinder track full-backs, not given to 'after you, Claude' niceties, but Bobby Charlton and some of his team-mates speak of them and other Bolton players with real affection and genuine friendship. One can only admire their awareness and consideration towards those affected by Munich, especially at this high point of their own Bolton careers."

So Roy and Tommy ended up doing their lap of honour after all but, while the story of their reticence seemed to confirm what I knew about Roy, it didn't exactly chime in with how I imagined Tommy Banks to be. Off the pitch, Roy has always been known as a naturally unassuming character but Tommy, as we shall see, would think nothing of standing up in front of a meeting of 300 fellow footballers and, with a few well-chosen words, swing the vote in favour of a players' strike.

Yet things are more nuanced than that. Tommy is undoubtedly a down-to-earth man but also a modest one, illustrated by something that happened after I'd interviewed him for this book. As we chatted in the street outside his house in Farnworth, a car pulled up and the young couple in it asked for directions to a nearby location. The driver was from Liverpool and there was immediate banter between him and Tommy about Bill Shankly. At one point I intervened to ask the driver if he knew that the man he was talking to quite by chance had been a top international footballer but, before I could get even halfway through the question, I was silenced by Tommy. Just as in 1958 he was quietly adamant that he wanted no fuss and the couple drove off no wiser about who they'd been chatting to.

The muted nature of the immediate post Cup Final celebrations was reinforced when a gracious Matt Busby limped into Bolton's dressing room to congratulate the team, Ridding and his backroom staff on their victory even before he'd been in to console his own players. "I want you to know the better team won," he told the Bolton dressing room.

Roy described Busby's entrance like this: "The first thing that came into my consciousness as he stepped through the door was how ill he looked. He was struggling to get round the dressing room and shake the hands of each player and his spirit and genuineness made me feel so small in my triumph. I still think he must have expended more energy and more mental and physical strength in coming to our dressing room than we had all produced throughout that tough ninety minutes. His resolution remains a wonderful memory of my footballing days."

In the hours after the final whistle blew, however, the mood of the Bolton camp picked up. Lofthouse stood to address the traditional celebration banquet in the glittering surroundings of The Café Royal to a huge ovation which became even more enthusiastic as he pointed out that the team had atoned for the 1953 defeat. The skipper then mixed compassion with pragmatism by adding: "We went into the final as the Other Team. This only gave us greater determination and, though we are sorry United could not crown their season with a win, football is a game where there can be only one winner and I am proud to say that team was Bolton Wanderers."

The celebrations went on to midnight with a cabaret which included appearances by comedians Tommy Trinder and Arthur Askey and Sinatra-lite crooner Dickie Henderson.

Then it was round the corner to fulfill the terms of a prediction famously made three months before. In February, after Bolton had beaten Arsenal 2-1, the club's first win at Highbury since 1929, Tommy Banks had led a delegation of euphoric Wanderers players into Soho, ending up at The Celebrity Club where he made his celebrated forecast. He remembers: "We told the manager, 'We're Bolton Wanderers and we'll win the Cup this year and afterwards we want to come here and bring our wives to celebrate.' " The Celebrity Club had absolutely no problem with that lucrative scenario and the manager promised the Bolton lads that, should they triumph, he'd reserve seats for themselves and their partners. Unfortunately, when they arrived at the club on Cup Final evening, the players found that others had had the same idea.

"We went and we couldn't get in," Tommy recalled. "The manager said, 'I'm sorry, Tommy, it's full of Bolton people.' "

Before long the party switched to their new base at The Great Western Hotel, in Paddington, where the teetotal George Taylor was dissuaded from going to bed and ended up acting as choir master during a rousing sing-song. The youngest member of the team Brian Birch, who was still doing National Service, had taken up the opportunity to link up with his family after the banquet. He returned to the hotel to find the place was jumping.

"I'd been out to meet my mother for a couple of hours," he told me, "and when I got back the party was in full swing."

Jean Edwards remembered the scene with a smile. "There was that much champagne," she said. "Tommy was drinking it out of his shoe." Tommy strongly contested this claim. "It was my wife's shoe," he told me.

The party went on until four or five in the morning – nobody is really all that sure – and ended with an early breakfast for a few die-hards in the foyer. One thing that is certain is that the amount they'd been allocated by the club for their celebrations was comfortably exceeded.

Barbara explained: "They'd said we could spend up to £50 at the bar. But we went mad – we had champagne and they weren't very pleased the day after when the bill came to £72. But we'd just won the Cup. And I wonder how much they spent going out! I wonder where they went. We didn't see them after the Café Royal."

"It was a fantastic night," remembered Roy, "I couldn't believe I was part of it."

Now £72 would doubtlessly have bought a fair bit of champagne in 1958 and - by the standards of the times - it was a truly boisterous evening. Yet, in its essence it was happy and all rather innocent – a marked contrast to the standards of some of today's players. A recent book shows the difference almost unlimited cash has made between footballers then and now. One extract concerns a trip by unnamed Premier League footballers to a nightclub called TAO in Las Vegas and the strange, completely bone-headed, competition that developed after these boys found themselves next to a table at which sat a number of "proper stars" including one from Barcelona. Here's what happened – and remember this lot aren't celebrating anything in particular.

"One of our party ... challenged them to a 'champagne war'. The idea is to send over a bottle of champagne; the other table is then meant to reciprocate, and on it goes until the bill gets too big for one side to pay. If a table keeps playing but cannot afford to pay, they are forced into the ultimate loss of face – they are marched out of the club by security to heckles and wolf whistles. The final bill? Just short of $130,000 excluding tip." That amount of bubbly would have filled a lot of ladies' shoes in 1958.

The following morning the team said goodbye to Birch who'd arranged a lift home to Southport with a pal before travelling straight on back to his base at RAF Dishforth in Yorkshire, where he worked as a telephone operator. Birch, who still had five months National Service to complete, said at the time: "Naturally I'm disappointed that I couldn't be with the lads. But I knew at least a week ago that I couldn't go back with them to Bolton. We are very short staffed on the station exchange and I have to get back on duty." It wasn't all work for Bolton's youngest finalist, however, as he would shortly be setting off on a tour of Yugoslavia with the RAF football team.

There was one final treat for the rest of the squad – a trip to see Sunday Night at The London Palladium. And while all agree that everyone was in a considerably less boisterous mood than the night before, memories of the event differ widely.

Barbara's recalled that Bruce Forsyth was in charge of proceedings. "He announced we were in the audience," she explained, "but nobody would put their hand up to go on stage. They didn't know where we were sitting either. Not a word was uttered." Roy chuckled at the memory.

However, Jean Edwards maintained it was Tommy Trinder who was master of ceremonies. "He wanted some of the players to go on stage to do that game, what was it, Beat The Clock? But nobody would go. I was willing to go but they wanted couples and Bryan wouldn't go."

Meanwhile Tommy Banks' take on proceedings is: "They had this competition to catch a ball in a top hat with a hole in the top and my wife were a rounders player and she were good with a ball. I said, 'Come on we're having this.' There were prizes – fridges, washers and all sorts – and she wouldn't go up. The only one who would go up was Barbara but I said, 'No, if I'm going up, Maggie's going up.' Tommy Trinder said, 'Come on, we're waiting for you,' but you couldn't cut a washer or a cooker in half could you?"

On the Monday morning Eddie Hopkinson travelled back up to

Hendon Hall to link up with the England squad preparing for a match against Portugal on the Wednesday. So only nine of the Final team started the train journey back to the North West from Euston. That figure went down to eight when the train reached Rugby and Tommy Banks was handed a telegram telling him to join the England party which would fly out to play internationals in Moscow and Belgrade in advance of the World Cup in Sweden in June.

Homecoming for the rest of the team was memorable for two reasons. The first was the mass of humanity which by early evening on Monday seethed around the blackened façade of Bolton Town Hall, stretching away down Newport Street from where the two single decker-buses carrying the team, directors, families and journalists approached. There must have been upwards of twenty thousand fans in and around that square. The other event of note had happened around an hour before as the buses made their way from London Road (now Piccadilly) Station in Manchester to Bolton.

As the bus, which had a hole cut in the top so players could look out, reached Irlams-o'th-Height it came under attack from a gang of children. One picture, headlined 'Cheyenne ambush pelts Bolton', shows Parry, Sproston, Gubbins, Taylor and Ridding with their heads down as the kids enthusiastically launched all sorts of debris at the coach. A largish missile can be clearly seen flying over the five men's heads and something large has just splattered on to the side of the coach. Characteristically, Roy was unfazed by the attack. "I can remember we were on the coach with the hood off and we got things thrown at us. Mind you, you get that don't you," he said with a chuckle. "It certainly didn't spoil the day. We'd forgotten it as soon as we were through Salford."

Haydn Berry, who was in the second coach, described the missiles as a "barrage of turf, tomatoes, flour and a few stones," but was keen to stress that the culprits were youngsters and added: "Elsewhere on the route people, many wearing United colours, applauded the Bolton team." The only injury reported in the paper was to seven-year-old mascot David Hartley whose hand was said to have been cut by flying glass from a window broken on the second coach. However, by the time the team and mascot are pictured lining up on the town hall steps in front of the crowd, David looks to have forgotten about his injury. And in a special Evening News supplement forty years later David doesn't mention the incident, although he does say that the police warned him that there might be trouble and urged him to stay in the coach. A news picture from the day shows David almost obscured by the Cup surrounded by players, including Roy in an almost Napoleonic pose, with his right hand tucked into his coat. Meanwhile Nat is thanking the huge crowd for their support. A heroes' welcome indeed.

The final Cup action of the campaign took place in the Midlands. The following month, after the players returned from a six-match tour of the continent, the club allowed Roy and Barbara to take the trophy to show to family and friends in Catshill, where the couple stayed with Roy's sister Joan and her husband George. Roy showed the Cup to children at his old school and later got a tremendous cheer from regulars and family members when the trophy was produced in a local pub, The Forest.

Roy's first football club was not forgotten either and the Cup was the attraction on the top table at Bromsgrove Rovers' annual dinner, where Roy and Barbara were guests. The local paper reports that Michael Higgs, the club president, jokingly referred to the Cup as "this small trinket." And Bromsgrove chairman, Mr D. G. Hughes added that they were very much indebted to their old player for "bringing the Rovers the nearest to the Cup they would ever get" and spoke of the pride at Rovers being mentioned in the Cup Final programme as Roy's first team.

It was a visit which, perhaps understandably, had its fraught element. Barbara explained: "We took the Cup in its big wooden box and were terrified of it getting lost. We even slept with it next to the bed and Roy kept waking up to check it was still there."

Roy added: "I can't believe they let us do that as there was only one FA Cup then. Can you imagine me going home with the FA Cup? It's another world. Barbara and I had the FA Cup with us. Beside the bed!"

ROY... with the famous trophy he took back to Catshill to show family and friends. (Bromsgrove Advertiser)

THE WINNERS... Nat proudly holds up the FA Cup to the delight of his team-mates, including Roy on the right in the picture.
(Bolton Evening News)

7

BACK STORY

I f, as popular legend has it, Roy Hartle was the best right back never to play for England, then who were the men who made sure he remained stuck with that unwanted title?

In the period between Roy making the right back position his own at Burnden in August 1955 and the end of England coach Walter Winterbottom's reign in November 1962 when Roy had recently turned thirty-one, there had been just three people standing in his way.

The first obstacle was the Birmingham City right back Jeff Hall who formed an effective partnership with Manchester United's Roger Byrne. In the seventeen games they played together England lost only once, and included a notable 4-2 victory against Brazil at Wembley in May 1956 in which the small and speedy Hall helped Stan Matthews tear apart the opposition's left flank. Both Hall and Byrne, having been wing-halves earlier in their careers, were as comfortable going forward as defending and would help to begin the redefinition of the full-back's role.

Yet something more significant and tragic links this pair; neither would reach his thirtieth birthday. As we've seen, Byrne died aged twenty-eight at Munich while Hall fell victim to one of the terrible scourges of Britain's post-war years. In March 1959 he was diagnosed with polio and died two weeks later at the age of twenty-nine. The passing of a young, fit footballer shocked the entire country and take-up of the Salk vaccine, which had been introduced in 1956, rose dramatically.

By that time Hall's England spot had been claimed by West Brom's Don Howe who, thriving under the tutelage of legendary manager and tactician Vic Buckingham, had developed into an overlapping full-back. Buckingham, who went on to manage Barcelona and Ajax, was an advocate of the non-stop pass-and-move system and encouraged Howe to always think of starting attacks.

Howe says that Buckingham, "stipulated ... that when our goalkeeper had the ball I should make myself available and demand the ball to set things in motion.

"Not only did he curb long-ball tactics in favour of more measured football but he also urged me to become an adventurous, over-lapping full-back. I credit him with helping me win a place in the England team at the 1958 World Cup."

Also in the England squad, although he didn't play in the tournament was the third and best player who was to stand in Roy's way. Jimmy Armfield developed what Hall and Howe had started and refined it to the point that by the next World Cup in 1962 he was rated the best right back in the world. And yet, the way Armfield tells it, his attacking role started almost by accident. Playing behind Stan Matthews for Blackpool, Armfield would watch as the opposition, in a desperate attempt to stop the old wizard, would pull their left winger back to double up in defence. This left a large empty space in front of him which Armfield was eager to fill and did so by charging forward to back up, and occasionally overtake, Matthews.

"I made it my job to impose myself on the opposition," said Armfield. "In the end the other teams were using players to mark me and it became more difficult."

Armfield's manager at Blackpool, Joe Smith, was however a bit more old school than Vic Buckingham. He preferred traditional full-backs like Eddie Shimwell, the man who Armfield replaced. When Smith, the captain of Bolton's first Cup winning team in 1923, saw his young defender charging, shoulders hunched, towards the opposition's bye-line, he was less than enthusiastic and made his feelings known. "He told me that our number seven (Matthews) was good enough," said Armfield.

Even when the tactic proved a success, Armfield says Smith was still not convinced and it was only after Ron Stuart became Blackpool manager in 1958 that overlapping runs were encouraged.

So there were formidable obstacles in the way of Roy's international career. And, while acknowledging Roy was a different type of full-back to himself, Armfield is keen to knock old stereotypes on the head. In fact the constantly repeated jokes about Bolton's full-back pair ("Chip him o'er here, Roy, when tha's finished wi' him.") seem to irritate the normally mild-mannered Armfield. "They're almost as bad as Bill Shankly stories," he told me and added: "Roy Hartle wasn't just a tough guy. He was a very good kicker of the ball. He could play. People like Roy and Banky were better on the ball than they were given credit for." So much so that from his position on the sidelines in Sweden, Armfield came to the conclusion that Tommy Banks was probably England's best player of the 1958 World Cup.

Perhaps if Roy had been a left back he would have stood more chance of international recognition. After Byrne's death in February 1958 until Winterbottom's final game in charge in November 1962 no fewer than ten footballers wore the number three shirt for England.

One left-back, albeit a newcomer at the time, reckoned Roy should have been given his international opportunity. "There were quite a few people in front of him like Jimmy Armfield," said Syd Farrimond, "but I would think that he deserved a chance. Sometimes you're lucky and sometimes you're not."

Roy is pragmatic enough to acknowledge that while he would have liked to have played for England, "I wasn't good enough for that." Especially given the talent standing in his way.

And yet you can still dream. "I kid myself when I'm smoking my pipe," he said in 2002, "I think, well, if Alf Ramsey had been in charge of the England team and not Walter Winterbottom when I was at my peak I might have had a better chance because Ramsey liked one or two fighters in the side. He had Nobby in and he had Bally ... and I thought I might have got through it a little easier. But Walter wanted finesse players and I can't say I was one of those."

So Roy had to be content with just one representative honour, an appearance for The Football League against the Irish League at Anfield in November 1958.

It's odd looking back, how much interest and comment this match generated. For a start the team was picked eight days before the game, allowing sports journalists to go to town on the selections.

Frank McGhee in the Daily Mirror was less than impressed with Roy's inclusion, given that these games were seen as unofficial trial matches for the senior England XI. While admitting the team would see off the Northern Ireland part-timers, McGhee added: "... it doesn't bear any resemblance to an England team of the future ... Though I respect their ability at club level, I can't see (Johnny) Wheeler or right back Roy Hartle winning caps in the future."

Haydn Berry, on the other hand, had no doubts about Roy's selection, saying: "It is his first honour as a professional footballer and well earned. Many supporters regard him as the most improved player on the staff."

Terence Elliott also backed the move, writing of Roy: "Selection approved emphatically ... could be on his way into the England side." He was less enthusiastic, however, about another Wanderer chosen for the match. Elliott wrote: "Why has the England inside forward trio (Bobby Charlton, Lofthouse, Johnny Haynes) that went to town against Russia at Wembley (all three had scored in the 5-0 thrashing, including a Haynes hat-trick) been chosen when this is a fine opportunity to groom up-and-comers into England stature. It looks all wrong to me." He went on to advocate Lofthouse's spot going to Len White, of Newcastle, Joe Baker of Hibernian or the 23-year-old Middlesbrough centre-forward Brian Clough.

In the event Elliott need not have worried as Lofty, who had scored six goals for the Football League against the Irish League in 1954, dropped out of the side with an injured knee and White, the stocky little ex-miner from Rotherham, took his place. Roy too was doubtful at one stage with a muscle strain but was eventually pronounced fit to play.

And he didn't disappoint that night at Anfield. Under a headline which said "Hartle shone in inter-league game," Haydn Berry reckoned: "International honours could soon be on the way for Roy Hartle ... after his competent and, in the second half, prominent display of his football wares. He revealed constructive play equal to anything seen from Alf Ramsey in his palmiest England days."

This positive view was echoed by Tommy Banks who was in the 30,717 crowd that night and agreed that Roy had had a very effective game just behind his old Bolton right-half partner Johnny Wheeler, who was now captain of Liverpool.

But the star of the show was undoubtedly Len White, who hit a hat-trick within eight minutes in a 5-2 win, the other goals coming from Haynes of Fulham and Liverpool's Alan A'Court. Yet White, who would finish as Newcastle's third highest goal scorer of all time behind Jackie Milburn and Alan Shearer, never gained full international honours. In a similar manner to Roy, Len White had to be content with an unofficial designation as the best uncapped English centre-forward of his generation.

8

ON THE BUSES

Three weeks after their daughter Beverley was born in Farnworth's Townleys Hospital on April 25th 1957, Roy and Barbara moved out of Woodgate Street. They were now living across town renting Nat's old house in Temple Road, Halliwell, the skipper and his family having made the celebrated move to the Castle Hotel in his home patch of Tonge Moor.

Lofthouse's stint as a pub landlord had brought him into conflict with the Wanderers, who initially refused permission for the move before relenting, somewhat reluctantly. The skipper actually lasted less than two years as a landlord before concluding he was not cut out for the business which, he reckoned, was not conducive to bringing up two children.

Roy and Barbara stayed in Temple Road for seven years, during which time their son Russell was born at Havercroft Maternity Home, in Victoria Road, Lostock, on October 20th 1959.

At twenty-five shillings a week rent, the new house was a definite step up from Woodgate Street. "It was a lot better up there," said Barbara. "It was a semi and nearly in the countryside. We weren't far from Smithills Hall." There were also more opportunities for outdoor pursuits, although one right outside their front door earned them a telling-off from neighbours.

"We went sledging with our friends next door during winter," said Barbara. "We put the kids to bed and took the sleds out on to the street. But we got told off by the few who owned cars because we were making the road too slippy. There's quite a slope going down."

At that point Roy did not own a car himself and that fact immediately highlighted one big disadvantage of the move away from Great Lever. It meant that instead of a ten-minute walk, Roy now faced a two-bus journey to Burnden Park - an arrangement which would last until the end of his career.

Barbara explained: "On match days Roy used to go before me because he had to be there at one o'clock. Sometimes I had somebody pick me up because Roy gave them a free ticket. I can't remember ever going on the bus, especially when we had two children, although sometimes I didn't take them."

Roy, however, has clear memories of using public transport to get to work. He said: "I used to catch the Halliwell bus into town and then it was the number eight from Bolton to Manchester. It was the normal thing to get on the bus. It didn't bother us."

This meant the Cup winner and Football League representative would find himself sharing trips into and out of town with fans making their way to Burnden to see him play. And though it kept him close to the people, Bolton folk, being as they are, weren't reluctant to tell him exactly what they thought of his and the team's performances.

"If you hadn't played well the supporters used to let you know about it," he said. "You couldn't get big-headed catching a bus. We'd take as long as we could after the game before we caught the bus home but there was always some wag on there who was going to have a go at you if things weren't going very well."

However, even the most miserable fans had little to complain about as the 1958-59 season opened with the Cup holders top of the table after six games, including emphatic home wins against Leeds United and Manchester City. Bolton were even convincing one or two influential voices that they were not a one-dimensional team. The News Chronicle's Midlands football reporter Charles Harrold, writing about Bolton's 1-1 draw with West Brom at the Hawthorns, thought Bolton's reputation as "a rough dirty side" was unwarranted. He said: "Bolton have a defence of strong characters physically but not once did they do anything which remotely suggested heavy-handedness ... Roy Hartle had a good match. He subdued (Derek) Hogg in a manner which few full-backs are able to do."

Bill Fryer in the Daily Express was even more enthusiastic about the apparent change in Bolton's style. After Wanderers beat Blackpool 4-0 in the middle of October, he wrote: "They showed ... that from a crowd of dashing, drab but willing workers they have become with experience together, a TEAM of quick strong craftsmen of high quality." He praised Roy and John Higgins for no longer taking "a kick-it-and-chance-it attitude" but instead passing the ball well and concluded, "Hartle is every bit as good as Don Howe." It was a theme Fryer had colourfully touched on in reporting Bolton's 2-0 home win against Birmingham City the previous month when he wrote "If Roy Hartle maintains progress you can expect him to join his jolly little pal Tommy Banks in the England full-backery."

The forwards too had struck a rich vein of form, particularly Lofthouse, who at the age of thirty-three, was playing out of his skin. Lofty's career was revived to such an extent that it merited an England recall for the 5-0 thrashing of the USSR in October in which he grabbed his last international goal to join Finney on top of the England scorers chart, with thirty apiece. He played his final international against Wales the following month.

Meanwhile on the back of huge personal success during the World Cup in Sweden, Tommy Banks continued his international career against Northern Ireland at Windsor Park in early October and, even though approaching his twenty-ninth birthday, he could reasonably have expected to have at least another couple of seasons playing for England. Unfortunately Tommy was injured in the match, missed the next five league games during which time Sheffield United's Graham Shaw came in at left back for the thrashing of the USSR and kept his place until the following May. Tommy's international career, which had lasted six games, was over.

The end of a chapter in one left-back's story was the start of another's. While Tommy was playing his final international in Belfast, Syd Farrimond made his debut for the Wanderers in a 0-0 draw against Preston during which, mercifully for him, he didn't have to mark the great Tom Finney who was also on international duty. "I was quite chuffed about that," he said.

That game at Deepdale was Syd's only appearance for the first team that season but in the following two terms he would play more matches than Banky, who was increasingly troubled by injury. In fact over his Bolton career Syd, who had played one game for an England youth side which included Bobby Moore, would partner Roy in almost fifty per cent more league and cup games than Banky (237 as opposed to 163). But the Hartle-Farrimond partnership did not get off to an auspicious start and left the youngster with an uncomfortable dilemma. Syd explained: "In one match I must have done something wrong because Roy had a go at me and I swore back at him. I was probably eighteen or nineteen and I wasn't a swearer as such but it was the heat of the moment. And I can remember I couldn't talk to him. I was thinking 'I shouldn't have done that.' Three or four days later in training I finally plucked up the courage to say 'I'm sorry' out of respect for him being a senior player. But Roy was OK about it and said, 'Forget it. It's gone.'"

If Tommy Banks's England career had ended prematurely there was better news on the international front that season for two other Wanderers stalwarts. Holden won the first of his five caps against Scotland at Wembley in April, a match that also saw the return of Hopkinson. The goalkeeper, dropped just before the World Cup after letting in five in a pre-tournament friendly against Yugoslavia, was brought in after Burnley's Colin McDonald broke his leg playing for The Football League in Dublin, an injury that would end his career. To complete the elevation of Wanderers to international level, Parry won the first of his two England caps later in 1959.

Bolton's early season explosive pace slackened off slightly but a blip of two defeats and a draw was ended emphatically by a 6-3 home thrashing of Manchester United in mid-November. The match was notable for a blanket of fog which descended on Burnden, obscuring at least half the pitch for many spectators. Not that the Bolton fans minded too much.

Thereafter Bolton were always hovering around the top four and after a 6-0 dismantling of Chelsea in early March, thanks to a hat-trick from young inside-right Freddie Hill, who was in for the injured Stevens, Bolton were eight points behind Wolves with three games in hand. The Wanderers couldn't press home their advantage, however, and despite four wins and a draw in the final six games they finished in fourth place, behind Arsenal who had the same number of points – fifty – but a better goal average. Nevertheless fourth spot was Bolton's best post-war finish and there had also been the bonuses of a 4-1 defeat of Wolves in the Charity Shield in October and a good cup run to the Sixth Round in which they were beaten 2-1 by Nottingham Forest at the City Ground.

The season may have been over but the club's footballing duties were far from at an end. For, as has already been seen with the 1956 four-match trip to Norway, this was the age of the club tour. It may seem difficult to believe that, while modern footballers earning millions complain about burn-out, their predecessors in the Fifties would play a string of matches abroad straight after the season had finished. And while some viewed the tours as directors' jollies, others embraced the idea. Roy was one.

Speaking before Bolton played their first ever competitive European tie against Lokomotiv Plovdiv in 2005, he recalled his own experiences. "You didn't even get into Europe for winning the FA Cup in my day and the only way we played there was in pre-season and end-season tours," he said. "We used to go away at the end of most seasons and I played in places like Barcelona and Real Madrid. I also remember the money which was a bit different from today. They used to give us £2 or £3 a day extra to spend. That was it! But we enjoyed those tours. Even though we only played friendlies there was an atmosphere and a buzz about playing European games."

Doug Holden was similarly positive, viewing the tours as a learning curve, although the lessons were sometimes harsh. He explained: "Players enjoyed going on tour at the end of the season to find out how other countries played but we found the rules were very different on the continent. You couldn't breathe on them. We toured Germany and were chased off the field by the crowd in one game."

This was the match against VfB Stuttgart in May 1960 which Bolton won 3-2 but angered the 5,000 spectators with what the Germans regarded as rough play. A Reuters' news agency report of the match reveals that the Wanderers were booed off but does not mention fans dishing out their own justice. However, the report does claim that Roy was sent off by the referee at the end of the match.

This news came as a shock to the Bolton party when they arrived in Seville four days later and read the report for the first time. Haydn Berry wrote about an incident just before the end of the match when Roy was the victim of "a vicious sliding tackle by the German inside right" but added "the subsequent get-together cleared the air completely," and the Bolton management vowed to take action to exonerate their full-back. The incident has hardly impinged on Roy's consciousness over the years as he can now remember little about it. And it didn't seem to affect him at the time as, in the next match against Seville, he played a blinder according to Berry, twice nearly scoring from thirty yards.

Maybe it was because he'd experienced life abroad with England, but Tommy Banks has far fewer enthusiastic memories of the post-season tours. "They were hard work," he said. "We went away for a fortnight and had to play four or five games. There used to be twenty-seven on the trip, thirteen players, Bert Sproston and Bill Ridding. All the others were directors and their wives. It didn't matter if you'd broken your leg you had to play. But it was a holiday for them."

For "a fortnight" read "six weeks" in the case of the tour to South Africa at the end of the 1958-59 season. Bolton played ten matches on the tour (winning eight and losing two) including two 'tests' against an amateur South African XI (both won) and travelled all over the country, finding time to marvel at the lions, elephants and giraffes in the Kruger National Park.

The team also had its first taste of the apartheid system with its bizarre and seemingly inexplicable social rules. Roy said: "I can remember you had to be on the opposite side of the road because of segregation. The black Africans could be on one side of the street and we had to be on the other.

"We were only kids really and we'd never seen anything like that before. I felt sorry for the black people because it was their country, after all."

The Wanderers players could not have known it but, as they strolled around the centre of Cape Town, less than a mile away in a community in the shadow of Table Mountain, another top sportsman was plotting his exit from South Africa – a move which would eventually help hasten the end of the apartheid system. Basil D'Oliveira, already a superstar in non-white cricket but unable to play for South Africa because of his colour, desperately wanted to test his skills in English conditions. And after enlisting the aid of the great BBC broadcaster John Arlott, he finally secured the job of professional at Middleton Cricket Club in the Central Lancashire League for the 1960 season. Six years later he was playing for England and two years after that his belated inclusion in the 1968 England party to South Africa led to the tour being cancelled and apartheid dragged into a merciless international spotlight under which it withered and eventually died.

That uplifting story is rightly celebrated to this day but what is less well-known is that the year after that football tour to South Africa, D'Oliveira turned out for Bolton Wanderers. According to Francis Lee, the great South African all-rounder played in a charity cricket match and his trademark big hitting nearly saw off one of the spectators.

Explained Lee: "We had a good cricket team and we played two or three charity games a year. That year one of our guests was Basil D'Oliveira. He'd only been here four or five weeks and I remember he hit the ball into the crowd. There was a woman asleep in a deckchair and it hit her on the forehead."

The year before that match, Lee had been a new fifteen-year-old ground staff boy at Burnden, waiting for the seniors' return from the southern hemisphere. And what his innocent ears heard shocked the young winger.

He said: "I joined in June 1959 and they'd just come back from the South African tour. I'd been working on the ground and painting and then I had to put the kit out for them. That was the first time I met them all. They were all sunburned and the most amazing thing is - in those days we never swore - all of a sudden these players came into the dressing room and they were swearing; every other word effing and blinding – you couldn't believe your ears! My parents never heard me swear until I was eighteen and that was a mistake. And the players were always taking the mickey out of each other."

The following season, 1959-60, looked like being enough to make any die-hard supporter swear. A terrible start with only one win in six matches was compounded by a catalogue of injuries. Lofthouse damaged his ankle ligaments in pre-season which put him out for the rest of the term. And a couple of games in, Roy was sidelined with a kidney injury sustained during a 3-0 home defeat against Blackburn.

Roy, who spent over a week in Newlands Nursing Home in Bolton, would be out of the team for seven games, his longest spell on the sidelines since returning to the first team at the beginning of the 1955-56 season. In the middle of October Tommy Banks damaged an ankle and was out until March, Edwards was injured in November and did not appear again that season. To cap it all, Hopkinson broke his leg during training in February and missed the rest of the campaign. The catalogue of woe could have spelled disaster in terms of league position. Yet, though goals were harder to come by in Lofthouse's absence, Bolton managed to finish in sixth position due to the second-best defensive record in the league.

With Stevens switched to centre forward, there was room for the young Freddie Hill to slot in at inside right, play virtually a full season and score eight goals. Another new name on the score sheet was that of Roy Hartle who notched five which, it has to be said, included four penalties. There was a new style of play too. For years the team had been conditioned to playing the ball first time to Nat so he could flick it on to other attackers with his head or receive passes down either wing channel and hold the ball up until help arrived. Now, with a new striker, there could be a bit more variation.

Doug Holden told me that he'd always wished the team had played more of a passing game and that season he got his wish with Stevens dropping deeper to receive the ball. "When Dennis played centre forward," said Holden, "we had to play it differently – into his feet. It was good football." Good enough for Bolton to finish sixth.

The following campaign began with Roy being named as club captain and given the unlikely role of centre forward as Bolton struggled for strikers. Lofthouse, who had reversed a decision to quit the game the previous January, was not yet fit for first-team action and his deputy Stevens was injured. So after three matches in which Parry wore the number nine shirt, it was decided that the new-look attack-minded Hartle would lead the line.

It was a move that had already occurred to some fans. In a letter to the Bolton Evening News, one wrote: "I wonder if Bill Ridding has ever considered Roy Hartle at centre-forward. The more I watch Hartle the more I'm convinced he is worth a trial at centre-forward when, perish the thought, Nat hangs up his boots."

Haydn Berry too was enthusiastic about Roy pulling on the number nine shirt in a night match against Wolves at Molineux on August 31st 1960. Berry reckoned: "The team's star penalty taker and frequent marksman nowadays with his dashes out of the defence ... is expected to add punch to a frail front line. Hartle has the height and weight that the Bolton attack badly needs (Wanderers had lost three out of their first four fixtures) but his selection is obviously only a temporary measure."

He could say that again. Bolton lost 3-1 and Roy was marked out of the game by the experienced Bill Slater. As he described it: "I had only two kicks that night, one on the shin and the other on the ankle. My crowning humiliation was the fact that Tommy Banks scored our goal." The experiment was never repeated. The following match Bolton's new £15,000 signing from Manchester City, Billy McAdams, wore the number nine shirt and scored two in a 4-1 win against Chelsea.

At the beginning of October Roy's predecessor as club captain, Nat Lofthouse, returned for what would be the first of his final half-dozen games for Bolton. After a few reserve matches, Lofty had demonstrated that he was over the ankle injury which had kept him out for the whole of the previous season. He made his comeback in a home match against Manchester United which is now memorable for a variety of reasons.

As well as Nat's comeback after seventeen months on the sidelines, it saw the league debut of a man who would play a key role for England during the World Cup in 1966, Nobby Stiles. No shrinking violet himself, Stiles remembers the awe with which he regarded the Bolton defence. Speaking of his debut, he said: "My own came in the X-certificate category because it was at Burnden Park ... and the Bolton defence read something like this, Hartle, Banks, Hennin, Higgins and Edwards. I remember thinking, 'You expect a team to have one hard man but this is ridiculous.' I felt like a pygmy when

I moved upfield and came up against this defence. It was a fantastic baptism into league football for me and … it was my first insight into the real hard men of soccer."

Pygmy or not, Stiles was influential in midfield and managed to lay on the equalising goal for eighteen-year-old Johnny Giles, later to become his brother-in-law and a kingpin of the fearsome Leeds United side of the mid-to-late Sixties and early Seventies.

Harry Gregg didn't get the chance to exact any revenge on Nat for his 1958 Cup Final charge. Instead the goalkeeper gave away a penalty when he brought down fellow Northern Ireland international McAdams, who had scored the first goal of the game. Gregg immediately redeemed himself, however, by saving Roy's spot kick with his feet after the full-back had blasted the ball straight down the middle, then jumping back to his feet and flinging himself sideways to divert a header from McAdams round the post. Roy, who had scored from the spot against Blackburn the week before but had missed another penalty in a 4-3 defeat by Everton seven days earlier, saw his spot-kick duties given to McAdams.

If Lofthouse was coming to the end of a brilliant career, another one was just beginning. Francis Lee, at sixteen not yet a full professional, was picked on the right wing for the match against Manchester City in early November. He had quickly lost any awe he might have had on the seniors' South Africa return and was now what Roy described as "a cocky little lad."

Yet, while brimming with confidence, Lee was sharp enough to realise that there were things he could not do, such as get on the wrong side of Roy Hartle. He said: "We would play practice matches against the first team players. I looked at Roy, with his big physical presence and me, a skinny nippy winger and I thought, 'He doesn't like wingers, I'd better keep away from him.' When I got into the first team, I quickly got used to playing against them. They were OK and wouldn't kick you – unless you took the mickey out of them."

That debut, a 3-1 defeat of City, encapsulated everything that was to come in Franny Lee's glittering career. In front of 34,000 people he scored a goal, took the corner from which Lofthouse headed another, and got himself booked for foul play. He also had a grumble at Lofty. Nat describes what happened after he'd headed in from Lee's cross: " 'Well done, Franny, nice ball,' I said, waiting for the congratulations. 'About bloody time, Lofty, the number of crosses I've put over,' came the reply. There I was over 20 years in the game, 33 England caps and a few goals to go with them, being firmly put in my place by a 16-year-old kid just starting out. I knew it was time to go!"

And, indeed, Nat had to put up with the younger man's moaning for just two more games. On December 17th 1960, against Birmingham City at St Andrew's, Bolton's lionheart centre-forward suffered an injury to his left knee and his illustrious twenty-one-year Wanderers career was finally at an end. During his time at the club, Lofthouse had experienced tragedy during the Burnden disaster of 1946 which claimed thirty-three lives; heartbreak when Blackpool snatched away his Cup Final dream in 1953 and triumph as he held the Cup aloft in 1958. He'd also scored a club record 285 goals in just over 500 games (it would have been many more but for the war) and been named Footballer of the Year in 1953, the year after he was dubbed The Lion of Vienna for his superbly brave England performance against Austria who, along with Hungary were the continent's finest team.

Roy says: "Lofty was unique. He was brave, more skilful on the deck than people gave him credit for and absolutely superb in the air. It was a pleasure and privilege to play in the same Wanderers team as him. He was a good friend too. There'll never be another like Nat."

From a personal point of view, it's the one big regret of my football watching life that I never saw Nat Lofthouse play.

But for the Wanderers, and for Roy who had taken over the captaincy from Lofthouse, there was no chance to dwell on the past as there was a relegation battle to win. Next to bottom of the league when Nat retired, the team put together a decent if unspectacular run after the turn of the year and managed to finish in 18th place. On the way they beat Cardiff 3-0 at home with Roy renewing his acquaintance with left-winger Derek Hogg, now playing for the South Wales side.

After one sortie into the Cardiff half when his cannonball shot struck the bar, Roy brushed Hogg aside and crossed the ball for Doug Holden to head in. One match report said: "Hartle – who emerged from his duels with Cardiff left-winger Hogg looking like the best right back in Great Britain – played a major role in a Holden goal." And in Bolton's final win of the season, a 3-1 home success against Nottingham Forest, Roy grabbed his second league goal of the season with a thirty-yard free-kick.

By the close of that season, with Tommy Banks on his way out of Burnden Park, the famous full-back partnership had come to an end. But a few months earlier it had provided one last sting in the tail. Since 1955-56, Hartle and Banks had together posed survival problems for First Division wingers. But now they were also instrumental in giving the game's vested interests a good kicking.

Between them Roy and Tommy played key roles in ensuring that by the mid-Sixties through the efforts of the Professional Footballers' Association, the English game was finally dragged into the Twentieth

Century. The two Wanderers defenders were crucially involved in the struggle to abolish the £20 a week maximum wage limit for footballers and introduce the most significant step in ensuring footballers' freedom of contract until the Bosman ruling of 1995. Typically Banky's intervention was flamboyant, funny and immediately effective while Roy's contribution was characteristically quieter, more persistent but, in the end, no less significant.

The Players' Union, as it was known originally, had been battling since 1909 for the abolition of the maximum wage which at that time stood at £4. Facing a strike threat by players, the Football League had agreed to introduce a bonus payment system but would not back down on the maximum wage, a position it broadly held until 1961.

There were other challenges to the system over the years but these were seen off, often with draconian measures. In 1948, England inside forward Wilf Mannion went on strike in a bitter dispute with his club Middlesbrough after it refused to supplement his maximum wage of £12 a week. Mannion was forced to back down or face being unable to play for England again. Another rebel, who never even got the chance to play for England, was Manchester United left winger Charlie Mitten. In 1950 when his Old Trafford contract expired he told the club he was joining fellow professionals Neil Franklin and George Mountford at Independiente of Santa Fe Bogota in Colombia, a country outside FIFA's control. The United manager Matt Busby was outraged. "You can't do that, you're not allowed to," he told Mitten, who ignored Busby and flew to South America.

Mitten was reportedly paid a £5,000 signing on fee and around £40 a week, a move which earned him the title of "The Bogota Bandit". However when Independiente ran into financial trouble, Mitten returned to England to face difficulties of his own. He was fined six months' wages and banned from the game for that time. He was also ostracised by Busby, who sold him to Fulham in December 1951. The business scuppered any chance Mitten had of international honours as well. Equally as heart-breaking was the case of Franklin, rated one of the best centre halves England ever had, who was banned from playing in the 1950 World Cup and never pulled on an international shirt again. When Franklin eventually returned from Colombia, he was given a four-month suspension.

By the turn of the Sixties the Players' Union had been re-branded as the Professional Footballers Association but the maximum wage was still in place, now fixed at £20 for senior players aged twenty and over, with an upper limit of £17 in the close season. Bonuses were set at £4 for a win and £2 for the draw. The PFA's larger-than-life chairman Jimmy Hill was now determined that this archaic restriction should be ended once and for all.

The matter came to a head at a key area meeting in the Grand Hotel just off Piccadilly, Manchester, in early January 1961 which attracted over three hundred footballers including Stan Matthews and Tom Finney. Hill chaired the meeting and, among the throng was the sixteen-year-old Wanderers junior Gordon Taylor, who like Hill would go on to lead the union. Taylor described how his senior club-mate and former coal miner Banky changed the direction of the meeting, which had been debating possible strike action.

Taylor explained: "The Bury delegate stood up and said, 'My father works down the pit and he doesn't get £20 a week. I think we need to be very careful about alienating the public and going on strike.'

"Then Tommy Banks stood up – everybody was hushed – and he said, 'Aye, Brother, I hear what tha sez. I've been down that pit and done tha Dad's job and I've got every respect for him. I know how tough it is. But I'll just say one thing. You try telling your Dad to come up out of that pit next Saturday afternoon and mark Brother Stanley Matthews and see what he has to say.' "

Banky remembered the intervention slightly differently. He said: "This lad from Bury stood up and said my Dad works in t'pit and I said, 'I can do what your Dad does behind my back. I were a coaler and I'll tell you this, there won't be thirty thousand watching your Dad spade coal. And there will be at Burnden Park.' And, with that, they all turned."

Chuckling at the memory, Taylor added that Banky's intervention brought the house down and the vote for strike action was almost unanimous. In the end there was no need for the footballers to withdraw their labour as the League backed down, the £20 upper limit was scrapped, and the Fulham chairman, comedian Tommy Trinder, had to wring as many laughs as he could from having to honour a promise to pay his star inside forward Johnny Haynes five times the old weekly maximum wage as Haynes became the first £100 a week footballer.

While all this was going on an equally significant drama had been rumbling on; a drama with a somewhat reluctant starring part for a skilful English inside forward and a vital supporting role for Bolton's other full back.

That inside forward, George Eastham, enjoyed four successful seasons at Newcastle United but by the end of the 1959-60 season had developed significant differences with the club over a variety of matters. With his contract due to expire Eastham told Newcastle he would not sign a new one and asked for a move which Newcastle refused, as they were able to do under the retain and transfer system. This enabled clubs to hold on to a footballer's registration and prevent him from moving. In a touch of supreme irony the manager of

Newcastle was Charlie Mitten, the Bogota rebel of ten years before whose attitude was, according to Eastham, "You don't play for us you won't play for anybody."

Eastham has described his struggle in these terms. "Our contract could bind us to a club for life. Most people called it 'the slavery contract.' We had virtually no rights at all. It was often the case that the guy on the terrace not only earned more than us – though there's nothing wrong with that – he had more freedom of movement than us. People in business or teaching were able to hand in their notice and move on. We weren't. That was wrong."

So, unlike the rest of his colleagues the following January, Eastham did go on strike at the end of the 1959-60 season and was out of the game until October when Newcastle finally agreed to sell him to Arsenal. However, both the footballer and the PFA thought the principle worth fighting for and, backed by the union, Eastham took Newcastle to the High Court in 1963, arguing that he had been subjected to an unfair restraint of trade.

Gordon Taylor described retain and transfer as "the big issue of the time" and went on to outline exactly what was at stake. "It would have bankrupted the union had we lost but we didn't; we won and Mr Justice Wilberforce declared retain and transfer *ultra vires* or beyond the law.

"Since that time if a club offered a player the same money he still had a right to go; if they offered him less he was literally free; if they offered him more they could ask for compensation. They set up a tribunal system under Lord Henderson and they put a fee on a player and it would gradually come down until he moved. So it was a massive decision and Roy was very much a formative part of that."

Roy, the Bolton Wanderers PFA delegate at the time, was a member of the union's executive committee from March 1962 to February 1967, a time described by the former PFA Secretary Cliff Lloyd as "its most important period."

Lloyd has pointed to the nuts and bolts work that went on after the Wilberforce judgment. In 1969, he explained: "There followed lengthy discussions to draw up a new deal over contracts which would be acceptable to both sides. Roy Hartle was a member of that committee which was responsible for drawing up the form of contract that is at present in operation."

In fact Roy was one of only four members of the PFA's executive allowed to appear on the national negotiations committee (the other three were Manchester United's Maurice Setters, Malcolm Musgrove of West Ham and Harry Leyland, the Blackburn Rovers defender).

Cliff Lloyd added that Roy was, "a level-headed, intelligent bloke. He may not say a lot at times but when he does, it is right to the point."

Gordon Taylor echoes Lloyd's judgment, describing Roy as "A very deep thinking man." In fact Taylor credits Roy with setting him on the path to his present role and a kind of national celebrity.

"He encouraged me to take over as Bolton's PFA delegate so I owe a lot to him," said Taylor. "He interested me in the union. Eddie Hopkinson took over from Roy and then I was pleased to do that job and it's led on to this. Roy talked about his time on the management committee with people like Malcolm Musgrove, Maurice Setters, Cliff Lloyd, who he had a high regard for, and Jimmy Hill. They were big names. So Roy helped shape my interest in the PFA.

"In those days the PFA was just Cliff Lloyd and a secretary. Now we've got four offices on this site (in Manchester), one in London, one in Birmingham and a staff of sixty."

Thanks to the work of people like Roy and his management committee colleagues the ground work was laid for more improvements during the Seventies, described by Taylor as "a massive period."

He explained: "We got a new standard contract and the right to move was improved. You could go straight away and the transfer tribunal would settle it afterwards. And eventually it all changed with Bosman where there was literal freedom at the end of a contract, apart from the youngsters. That's where we are today."

And even if supporters can make a compelling case against paying mediocre present-day Premier League players £100,000 and more a week, it's almost impossible to argue that the ending of the maximum wage and lifting the restrictions on contracts were not beneficial developments.

PFA work was not the only extra-curricular football-related activity in which Roy was involved at this time. Over a week in the middle of June 1960 he attended a course at Lilleshall National Recreation Centre in Shropshire to gain his Preliminary FA Coaching Certificate. A month later, a letter from FA Secretary Sir Stanley Rous revealed he had been successful, with "satisfactory" grades in practical coaching and performance and "passes" in theory of coaching and laws of the game. The preliminary badge allowed Roy to coach secondary age schoolboys in preparation for taking the exam to gain his full certificate. Over the following season his afternoons were spent at various educational establishments in the Bolton area, including Barbara and Nat's old school, now known as Castle Hill County Secondary. The following June Roy was back for another week at Lilleshall in a bid to gain the full coaching certificate. And among the sixty or so footballers or ex-players aiming for that qualification were some famous names. They included Don Revie and Bertie Mee, both of whom would win the League and FA Cup in the next decade with

Leeds United and Arsenal respectively. Jack Charlton was also taking the first steps on a coaching career which would see him lead the Republic of Ireland to the World Cup quarter-final in 1990.

At the same time, sixteen other qualified coaches were taking an advanced refresher course. They included Tommy Docherty, then player coach of Chelsea, Roy's PFA colleague Malcolm Musgrove and another West Ham player Phil Woosnam, who was to have a crucial role in the development of football in the USA. This, as we shall see, made him partly responsible for the first (and last) foray into senior coaching by Roy Hartle, whose award of the full certificate was confirmed by the FA the following month.

9

FOOTBALL –
BUT NOT AS WE KNOW IT

This is the part of Roy's story where I can begin to contribute from experience – and make a confession as embarrassing as the one about never seeing Nat play. Shockingly, I didn't really get involved in watching football until I was the advanced age of nine-and-a-half when most of my contemporaries were already fervent devotees of the Trotters.

Family background can't be blamed either as my Dad, uncles and an aunt were keen Wanderers fans and had been to Wembley to watch both of Bolton's Fifties Cup Finals. I'd even been presented with a programme from the 1958 match – which I'd promptly discarded. Thinking back, I can only put it down to imagining that professional football was just an extension of the grim stuff I played in during school games on Great Lever Park. A line of kids, short-back-and-sides heads down, chasing a heavy sodden ball like iron filings drawn to a magnet. All that changed on May 6th 1961.

If that day was a beginning for me, it was an end for my Dad who for over twenty-five years had been a top-class wicket keeper for a number of local cricket clubs and held stumping records in both the Bolton League and Bolton Association. He picked up fifty-six victims for Tootals SC in 1951, a Bolton Association record at the time and four years later took forty-nine catches and stumpings for Farnworth in the Bolton League, still the club's best achievement by a wicket-keeper.

Dad enjoyed his time at Farnworth and became great friends with their West Indian professional Ken Rickards, a loyalty that later played havoc with his rational thought processes. For many years my Dad insisted that Rickards was a better cricketer than Garfield Sobers, with whom he'd also played - albeit very briefly - at Radcliffe. He stuck to his guns even into the late Sixties when Sobers became the world's greatest all-rounder with an eventual batting average of 57.78 from ninety-three Test matches. By contrast Ken Rickards played in two Tests, averaging 34.66 with the bat.

Nevertheless I'm proud to declare that Rickards was a guest at our terraced home in Eustace Street a few times, although I can't say I remember the visits with any clarity. However one of my earliest memories does concern Farnworth Cricket Club and I can still recall with a shudder how I was encouraged (at gunpoint?) to sing Rudolf the Red Nosed Reindeer on stage in the clubhouse at Farnworth's ground, Bridgeman Park.

At the start of the 1961 season, however, Dad was turning out for the other local cricket team in Farnworth. He was playing his first, and as it turned out his last, game for the Bolton Association side Farnworth Social Circle at Walker Institute. I'd gone along to watch as Walkers wasn't far from where we lived but it soon became clear nobody would seeing too much cricket that day. After a few balls the heavens opened and that was it. All was not lost, however, as Dad and a few of his new team-mates decided that they might as well descend on our house and watch the Cup Final, Leicester City v Tottenham Hotspur, on television. The move also solved my mother's dilemma of what to do that afternoon. She'd been at a bit of a loose end so the prospect of making a ton of sandwiches for hungry cricketers was no doubt a welcome distraction.

The 1961 Cup Final was the first proper match I'd ever seen on television, or anywhere for that matter. I'd somehow managed to miss an early attempt to televise league football eight months earlier in September 1960 when the ITV cameras came to Bloomfield Road to capture Bolton's 1-0 early evening win over Blackpool thanks to a goal from Freddie Hill. So the Leicester v Spurs match was the first match I'd witnessed – and what a revelation it was!

For a start, everybody on the pitch seemed to have a pre-planned position, few if any of the players ran around like headless chickens and not one of them propelled the ball with the large heavy toe-cap of his boot, mainly because they all seemed to be wearing slippers. In other words it was quite unlike anything I'd ever experienced. Occasionally I would glance surreptitiously at the adults in our living room to see if they were in as much wonder as I was at the spectacle but if they were they didn't show it. It helped of course that Spurs were the pre-eminent side of those times, already league champions and about to become the first double winners of the Twentieth Century. And my enjoyment of the match was hardly hindered by the fact that it was played on a flat Wembley surface and controlled by players who could stroke the ball around with nonchalant ease.

It did help that Spurs were playing against virtually ten men, after the Leicester right-back Len Chalmers suffered a serious injury midway through the first half and was a passenger for the rest of the match much in the way that Eric Bell had been in the 1953 Final. I can't recall what was on my Mum's sandwiches that day but I can clearly remember the goals, the first a shot on the turn from stocky curly-haired Spurs and England centre-forward Bobby Smith and the second a header from winger Terry Dyson which ended with the ball in the net and Leicester's athletic young goalkeeper Gordon Banks wrapped around the post. Like Bobby Charlton in 1958, Banks would recover from this disappointment to find himself in a considerably happier position on the same ground five years later. By the time the match ended and the Spurs captain Danny Blanchflower held up the silver trophy that had lain in its wooden box beside Roy and Barbara's bed in Catshill three years before, I was hooked.

Dad's increasingly arthritic knees ensured his Farnworth Social Circle career ended almost before it had begun and meant he had played his last cricket match at the age of forty. However, he did remain mobile enough to take me to see Spurs when they came to Burnden Park the following October. In the years since I've puzzled over why, after being so captivated by my first glimpse of professional football, I did not rush down Weston Street to Burnden on August 19th for the first match of the 1961-62 season, a goalless draw against Alf Ramsey's newly-promoted Ipswich. It can't have been worries about contrasting styles. I had yet to formulate the notion that Bolton played a, let's say, slightly less cultured brand of football than Tottenham. Or Ipswich for that matter. Frank Taylor, the only sports journalist to survive the Munich air crash, showed his impatience at the "cheerless" spectacle served up by the two teams that afternoon. "Ipswich played it sweet and slow," he wrote. "Click, click, click – rather like watching an industrious ladies' knitting circle at work, so neat, dainty and precise ... and just about as punchy." Meanwhile Bolton, "tried to play it fast and furious but most of the shots were in danger of felling the floodlight pylons."

A match to miss then, although I can't claim that I had prior knowledge that Bolton v Ipswich was going to be such a joyless experience. No, I'm ashamed to admit that I didn't go to that first game of the new season because I was still fixated on that Spurs team

- an early manifestation of celebrity culture which gripped me totally. Spurs had been on the telly and that made them special.

When I finally did walk down Weston Street, under that low railway bridge where the double-decker buses still became stuck, I entered a magical world that has gripped me ever since. The first thing I noticed when Dad and I came up the tunnel and on to the Burnden Paddock was the lights. By modern standards Bolton's floodlights, which had been first switched on exactly four years before, were woefully underpowered. But to someone who had never seen things lit up in this way anywhere, they were awesome and fully deserving of the oft-repeated claim that they possessed sufficient power to provide street lighting from Burnden Park to Bloomfield Road, Blackpool.

Then there were the players' shirts which seemed to shimmer in the artificial light, giving fantastic contrast between the glowing white of Bolton and dark blue away strip of Spurs. After becoming a regular at Burnden I always thought that the old gold of Wolves was the strip best suited to lights and certainly football kits have never looked as good to me again, especially now that every other fan wears one to the match.

The smells were different too. Roy noted that on his debut he remembered the distinctive aroma of Christmas cigars drifting across the pitch. That October the smell was more Woodbines, Park Drive and Capstan full strength cigarettes, the burning ends of which glowed like fireflies all round the ground. Burnden Park was still a proper football arena as well. The Great Lever End had not yet been given over to ugly blue plastic seats bolted to the terrace. And the Embankment or Bolton End was still exactly as it was when Liverpool comedian Arthur Askey stopped his train on the adjoining line to watch a game in the 1954 film comedy classic The Love Match.

This was, of course before our famous Embankment was chopped in half during Bolton's lost decade, the 1980s, by the building of a superstore, which made it appear as if a big ugly lorry had lost its way and reversed into the ground. But in the early Sixties Burnden was still capable of holding more than twice the crowd of 24,726 that had been attracted by the visit of the double winners.

I'm proud to say that I was on the Great Lever End the last time there were 60,000 spectators crammed into Burnden - for the FA Cup Semi-Final of 1966 in which Everton beat Manchester United 1-0 with a goal from Toffees newcomer Colin Harvey. I can clearly remember being frightened and exhilarated at the same moment as a great wave of bodies, including my own, tumbled forward as the ball flew into the net past Nat's old pal Harry Gregg. The previous season, Bolton's Fifth Round match against Liverpool had attracted a crowd of 57,207. It was the only time I can remember fans parking in our road, which was nearly a mile away from Burnden, (we'd moved from Eustace Street by then). And that was in an era when car ownership was by no means universal.

Back in October 1961, however, at my first live football match, I'm ashamed to say I was more excited by seeing the Spurs team than Bolton. I was canny enough not to actually shout for Tottenham but had no trouble recognising the figures I had first seen as small grey shapes flickering across our television screen. Now here they were in glorious Burnden-to-Blackpool floodlit colour. That tall elegant figure at right-half could only be Blanchflower and the character alongside his skipper in midfield was unmistakably Dave Mackay, for whom the description "barrel-chested" could have been patented. Mackay is one of the few players who can be mentioned in the same breath as Roy Hartle as one of football's hard men of those times. If you doubt it, take a look at the iconic photograph in which a snarling Mackay has grabbed a handful of football shirt, inside which is imprisoned an extremely nervous-looking Billy Bremner, not generally a player who backed down from a confrontation. As left-half, Mackay would most likely have found himself in the same part of the pitch as Roy some time during the game but neither Roy nor I can remember any confrontation that night. What Roy did say, however, is that Mackay, "was a terrific player, strong, brave and very skilful. He was a tremendous opponent."

I suppose I could gild the lily and say that my eye was particularly caught by Bolton's 6ft 1in tall, muscular and very determined right-back but the truth was that to me Roy was just one of the players in the drama that night who did his bit to make Bolton determined opponents to a classier side. In the end they were overcome but by only two goals to our one, scored by Freddie Hill, who was being watched that night by the Liverpool and Everton managers Bill Shankly and Harry Catterick.

If I'd been paying less attention to Blanchflower, Mackay, Johnny White and Cliff Jones that evening I might have noticed that the Bolton team was in the process of undergoing a change as profound as that of the mid-Fifties when the youngsters in the Central League side started to come through. Now their turn had come to be displaced. No fewer than five of the 1958 Cup winners had left the Burnden scene at the end of 1960-61 and in later years I would have real regrets that I saw none of them play. Lofthouse had finally retired barely halfway through the previous season; Banky had dropped out of the league altogether to play for Altrincham; Hennin was down the road at Chester; Higgins had moved to Wigan Athletic, then a non-League club; and Parry, the hero of that Sixth Round epic against Wolves was by the seaside, already impressing Blackpool fans with his sweet left foot.

Also not playing in that match against Spurs were Birch and Holden and of the four Cup winners who did turn out, Stevens would be on his way to Goodison Park the following March, where he would play a key role in Everton winning their first league title for twenty-four years. The other three remaining Wembley men were Hopkinson, Edwards and Hartle, who would very soon become big favourites of mine. Standing in for the injured Holden that evening, in just his ninth league game, was Franny Lee, the cocky lad who had taken the Lion of Vienna to task. I took particular notice of him because at seventeen he was the youngest player on the pitch and already provoking terrace controversy between those who thought him a real prospect and others who reckoned that, while he showed undoubted promise, he'd never be as good as their favourite, Holden.

By the time I walked back up Weston Street at about twenty-past nine that night my very brief flirtation with the glory, glory boys of Spurs was over. In its place was a desire to make up for lost time and get to grips with all things Wanderers, starting with naming the team. By the following morning when I was trying to impress schoolmates with the fact that I'd been to the match – none was too bothered as most had been going to Burnden for years – I was word-perfect on the Wanderers line-up. I still am. It was Hopkinson, Hartle, Farrimond, Stanley, Edwards, Rimmer, Lee, Stevens, McAdams, Hill, Pilkington.

Bolton were away to Blackpool and Ray Parry on the following Saturday – another 2-1 defeat – but the weekend after that we were at home to Wolves for my first Saturday match. This time I was largely indifferent to the opposition but I can remember one or two of the Wolves boys who looked good, particularly the half-backs Eddie Clamp and Ron Flowers either side of centre-half Bill Slater, who had impressed Tommy Banks with his marking of the Brazil play-maker Didi during the 1958 World Cup – and who had made Roy's one game at centre-forward such an ordeal.

Young Franny Lee's three-match run in the firsts had come to an end and he was replaced by the crowd's favourite Holden, back after six games out with injury. OK he was a bit ring-rusty but I could see immediately what they were all going on about. Holden had skill to burn. As did the youngster Freddie Hill, a smooth as silk operator who was only a year away from his England debut. Team skipper was centre-half Bryan 'Slim' Edwards, who never seemed ruffled and usually wore a half-smile which suggested he was enjoying a rather good joke that nobody else was in on.

Behind the skipper was Eddie Hopkinson in goal. I was particularly interested in him because I had ideas about being a goalie and was keen to pick up tips. And you could hardly have had a better role model than Hoppy. He was quick, fearless, a great shot stopper and never stopped talking to - or moaning at - his defence. Hoppy's only drawback was the fact he was just 5ft 8in tall but he always managed to counter this disadvantage with simple physics. Before every opposition corner you'd see him just off the pitch, hanging on to the far post at arm's length. As the corner came over he'd pull hard on the upright to propel himself forward like a clay-pigeon springing out of the trap and hurtle through the air at the approaching ball. He'd catch it too more often than not – and he rarely wore gloves. Instead he rubbed resin on his palms, "which helps get your hands stuck round the ball," he explained.

Should the fans tire of watching Hoppy they could always turn their attention to the character in the crowd behind the goals who mimicked the 'keeper's every move, diving saves, bollockings and all. When Hoppy spat on his hands as he prepared for a corner so did this guy. He probably had the full kit on under his overcoat, waiting for the call that never came. The only thing Hoppy couldn't do well was kick the ball a great distance but, to be fair, few could in those days. Tommy Banks reckons the reason Stan Hanson's career in the Bolton goal lasted so long was that he was a brilliant kicker of the heavy old T ball. "He could kick it over the halfway line from a goal kick and there weren't many could do that," said Tommy.

Then there was 'Chopper' Hartle. If you stood by the wooden fence on the Lever End right next to the high metal gate that divided it from the Burnden Paddock, you'd have a close-up of what the left-winger was up to. In those early days of mine, if Bolton were playing with their backs to the town centre then you'd be able to gauge how tricky Bolton's Brian Pilkington could be or, as an occasional treat, marvel at the manner in which Doug Holden kept his standards up a decade after first appearing for the Wanderers. If Bolton were facing the embankment then you could watch how the opposition's left-winger dealt with the threat of Roy Hartle. Usually descriptions of encounters like this are couched in terms of the damage a skilful winger can do to the opposing defence but things were rather different at Bolton in the early Sixties. Given that the Burnden pitch was built up to a height of three feet, the eyes of kids lining the fence would be about level with the winger's knees, usually the first parts of his body to hit the ground after a challenge from Roy. It's often said that the pitch was built up on cotton bales and old barrels and you can imagine a tackle from Roy was like being hit by a keg full of dark mild – come to think of it, a couple of adjectives that perfectly sum up Roy's dual character.

The match after Wolves was against Manchester United at Old Trafford and, as at that stage I didn't go to away games, I missed a satisfying 3-0 win for the Wanderers. But I was there at the next home match against Sheffield United to witness one of Roy's rare goals, a quickly-taken deflected free kick which flew past former England goalkeeper Alan Hodgkinson. Goals were proving easier to come by than the previous season so it was a blow when the team's prolific centre-forward Billy McAdams, the man who had ably taken over from Nat, was transferred to Leeds. In just fifteen months at Bolton he had notched up an outstanding twenty-nine league and cup goals in fifty-two matches. In the following match at Ipswich, Roy endeavoured to assume the scoring duties with Bolton's two best shots at goal but it was in defence that he won plaudits from a distinguished source.

Reporting on the match, John Arlott, wrote: "Over it all towered the figure of Hartle. He lifted full-back play to heights of imaginative perfection, shutting out Leadbetter, kicking a precise length, often acting as an extra outside-right and, for good measure, delivering two of the best shots of the game."

It's to Roy's great credit that he received such praise from a legendary sports journalist but it masks the fact that Bolton lost the match 2-1 to a team on its way to winning the League Championship, steered there by Alf Ramsey, the man who would deliver English football's greatest moment four-and-a-half years later.

Stevens took on centre-forward duties again after McAdams' departure so it came as a shock to me and many other fans when he too left the club in late February for Everton in a £35,000 deal. Harry Catterick, the Everton manager, decided to use Stevens in a deeper-lying midfield role and would be rewarded for his tactical nous with the League Championship the following season, a campaign in which Stevens played a crucial role.

A couple of days after Stevens left the club, the Wanderers signed from Wrexham a man who became my first real footballing hero, Wyn "The Leap" Davies. He was a nineteen-year-old Welshman who, it was said, could barely speak a word of English when he arrived in Bolton. Not that I or any of my footballing mates, clamouring for his autograph after training during the Easter holidays, cared about his linguistic skills. The only thing that mattered about Big Wyn was that he could out-jump any centre-half and propel the ball with enormous force, using his powerful neck muscles.

Davies put those muscles to good use during the highlight of that first season of mine as a Wanderers fan, a 6-1 thumping of Nottingham Forest in the middle of April in which he was one of six scorers. Apart from my obvious delight, the only detail I clearly remember about that match was that the Forest goalkeeper with back-ache that day had the comedy surname of Grummitt. That victory began a sequence of four wins out of the last five games to leave Bolton finishing in eleventh place, a considerable improvement on the previous season. Not bad, I thought, for my Wanderers baptism. Luckily my ten-year-old self wasn't to know that top-flight position would not be bettered for another forty-two years.

With the departure of Holden to Preston in October 1962, Roy and team captain Edwards were now the senior figures in a team that was rapidly assuming a more youthful look. Lee made the number seven shirt his own for a significant part of the season; Hill, almost a veteran by now at twenty-two, was rewarded for his skilful displays with two England caps. Later in the season in a match against Sheffield United

Bolton would field their youngest ever forward line, with Lee and Hill joined by twenty-year-old Davies, Denis Butler, aged eighteen, and sixteen-year-old inside forward Brian Bromley. Highlights of the early part of the season were a 3-0 defeat of Manchester United in front of 45,000 people at Burnden and beating Spurs 1-0.

I can't remember why, but I watched that match for the first and only time from the Wing Stand, a structure shoe-horned into the corner of the ground where the Great Lever End met the Manchester Road stand. This time it wasn't the Tottenham line-up that interested me, even though the Spurs players were even more familiar to everyone due to their televised European Cup exploits the season before. The London club had reached the semi-final of the competition before going out to the eventual winners Benfica. That didn't bother me any more. What was of more concern was whether Franny Lee, Wyn Davies or maybe Freddie Hill could unlock that celebrated Spurs defence before the prolific Jimmy Greaves managed to get onto the score-sheet. In the event it was none of these names who grabbed the decisive goal in the dying minutes. Instead Bolton's twenty-four-year-old inside left Peter Deakin, against the run of play, collected a pass from Hill, side-stepped the defender and fired the ball low past Bill Brown in the Spurs goal. It was Deakin's finest moment in a Wanderers shirt – and, up to that point, my favourite as a fan.

That match against Spurs was notable for another reason; it was the last before Bolton went into an unscheduled but extended mid-season break due to the icy weather. The only match played by the club between December 8th and March 6th was at Highbury where Arsenal had under-soil heating. This game, on February 16th 1963 finished 3-2 to the Gunners.

After the break Lee resumed his place on the right wing and began to delight in helping put even more wind up opposing left-wingers. "One trick we used to have," he explained, laughing at the memory, "was that if a winger was receiving the ball with his back to Roy I'd shout 'in hard, Roy,' and they used to jump. Of course, Roy would be about fifteen yards away."

He wasn't laughing, though, when Roy tore a strip off him for making him dash fifty yards in vain. Lee takes up the story. "I'd got the ball and I could hear Roy thundering down the wing and I thought I'll run towards the full back and then flick it on his outside so Roy can take one touch and cross it. And he's nobody to beat. Everything went to plan until I flicked it on the outside - and it went behind Roy. He went mad and gave me such a bollocking."

Another player who made his first appearance against Wolves that season was Gordon Taylor, the star-struck lad who along with many others had been so captivated by the Sixth Round classic between the two clubs in 1958. After he'd been given an England schoolboys trial, a number of clubs including Arsenal, Birmingham and Preston were interested in signing Taylor. North End even invited him to Deepdale to see Tom Finney's final match, against Luton Town in 1960. But the young winger's mind had already been made up, as he explained. "I went to Bolton because my Dad knew George Taylor. They'd been to the same school in Ashton and my Dad used to get tickets off him. I saw virtually all the games apart from the final when they won the Cup in '58."

The emergence of young stars like Lee and Taylor, plus the other new forwards and the likes of defender Dave Hatton was exciting and encouraging. But it could be argued that players with valuable experience had been jettisoned prematurely. Nowhere was this more emphatically demonstrated than at Goodison Park on May 4th 1963 when Bolton, in the middle of a run of defeats, struggled to contain an Everton side five games away from picking up the league title.

To add insult to injury, at the heart of their midfield behind the Golden Vision Alex Young and goal machine Roy Vernon, was Dennis Stevens, not yet thirty and playing as if he'd never been anywhere else. I can speak about this game with some authority as it was the first away match I'd been allowed to attend – with the proviso that I was accompanied on the train journey by my uncle. One of my most vivid memories is of the music played over the tannoy before the match and at half-time, and the contrast it provided with what we were used to at Bolton. While Burnden would echo to the dreary thump, thump, thump of The Liberty Bell brass band march (the Monty Python theme tune before they added the raspberry), Goodison Park was bouncing along to the latest single from an up-and-coming local combo.

"That's them Beatles, that is," I was informed authoritatively by my Uncle Tom as most of the 52,000 crowd roared along with From Me to You. And there was I under the impression it was a debut single from The Chuckle Brothers.

Another abiding memory was the state of the Goodison pitch – brown and almost grassless after something had apparently gone badly awry with the under-soil heating system. There was little wrong with the Everton team, though and Bolton did well to hold out until the 72nd minute when Vernon scored the only goal of the game. From memory, Roy kept the Everton left-winger Derek Temple comparatively quiet but it didn't really matter as the rest of them ran riot, particularly the right-winger Alex Scott, known to the crowd as Chico.

I travelled home invigorated by my first visit to Beatleville, as

Kenneth Wolstenholme would christen it on the first Match of the Day the following year, but chastened enough to realise that the defeat put Bolton in deeper relegation trouble, a situation hardly improved by a 4-0 home setback against Sheffield Wednesday a couple of days later. Luckily the drastically rearranged fixture list immediately threw up two more home matches, against Leicester and Liverpool, in the final three games and we managed to win both and finish three places above the relegation zone in 18th.

There was to be little respite, however. Ten defeats in the first thirteen games of the 1963-64 season set the tone for a disastrous campaign which would end Bolton's twenty-nine-year spell in Division One. The team was beset by poor form and injuries from which even the tough and consistent Roy Hartle was not immune, although in this instant his nemesis was not a rugged left-half or spiteful winger – but his four-year-old son Russell, taking a breather from one of the robust games they played.

Barbara explained: "Roy had a habit of switching the lights off and chasing Beverley and Russell around the house. How they didn't fall downstairs I do not know. But this particular time he was just messing around with Russell on his knee and he scratched Roy's cornea with his nail. Roy said, 'Gosh that hurt' and he had to go to the infirmary where they put the biggest bandage on his eye I've ever seen."

The injury was serious enough to put Roy out of a Fourth Round FA Cup match and replay against Preston and the fear of god up Russell. Speaking from a perspective of fifty years, Russell recalled "the infamous poke in the eye". He said: "Just like now with me and my daughter Francesca *(born in 2010)*, my Dad and I 'toy fought' most nights. But an accidental finger went astray and I put Dad out of an FA Cup tie. Every time the doctor came to see my Dad, regarding the eye, I ran upstairs because I thought he would tell me off for injuring my Dad."

However, as far as the manager was concerned, Russell was in the clear. He knew who was to blame. Barbara recalled what happened when the story made it into the national press. "All the reporters came and they were up in the bedroom," she said. "Then Bill Ridding walks in and says, 'Don't believe her, she did it. Not Russell.' I know he was only joking."

However, both Barbara and Russell are exonerated by Roy who takes all the blame. "We were fooling around," he said. "I should have known better."

The poke in the eye had not forced Roy to sit out any league matches – he would miss just one all season – and it's to his credit he never used the injury as an excuse for what happened three weeks later when he came up for the only time against arguably the finest British player of his generation. No, the problem Roy had with George Best that night at Old Trafford, February 19th 1964, was not seeing the man, but catching him.

Roy remembered the occasion with awe. "There was this lad, seventeen years old and he probably didn't weigh nine stone. I thought, this is terrible to play against him; it's not fair on the lad really. He's five foot seven, five foot eight, weighs in about nine stone and I'm clocking in at about twelve, twelve and six foot. And I never saw him! He absolutely ran me to death. People don't associate George Best and myself, thinking that I am so much older than him but I actually had the honour to play against him – if you can call it that!"

Roy can console himself that he wasn't entirely to blame for his performance that night. Gordon Taylor, by now established as a first team regular, explained that Ridding's tactics left something to be desired as well. "Bill gave the team talk," said Taylor, "and said we had to concentrate on Bobby Charlton, Denis Law and David Herd down the middle. He said they only had two young wingers from Northern Ireland so he wanted the full-backs, one of whom was Roy, to cover the centre backs because it was all going to come down the middle."

Well it didn't. Three minutes into the match, Best beat Roy on the outside and crossed to the near post where the ball flew into the net off left-half Dave Lennard. In the 57th minute Roy pulled Best down in the penalty area and Law fired the penalty wide. The miss didn't bother United who were already two-nil up and added to Bolton's misery shortly afterwards when Best put the ball on a plate for Law to score the third. Charlton, with a twenty-yard smash from a free kick, and Herd completed the scoring with Bolton counting their blessings it wasn't many more.

Only Hopkinson's skilful and brave goalkeeping kept the score down to extremely embarrassing rather than downright terrible. It was Roy's twenty-first game against United and definitely the most humbling. Yet he could look back on more wins (ten) than defeats (nine) although the fact that seven of those victories came in the first nine games showed the different directions in which the two clubs were heading.

By contrast Taylor was playing just his second match against United. It was his first appearance at Old Trafford and he made the mistake of going past Denis Law and ignoring the Scot's warning not to do it again. He did it again and, according to Taylor, ended up in the dressing room with the United team doctor treating him for a broken nose. To disorientate him even further, Bill Ridding appeared and began to act very oddly.

Taylor remembered: "I told him, 'I'm OK, boss, and I want to get back on' – there were no substitutes in those days. But he said, 'It's my job to look after your welfare,' and I thought it was a bit odd because usually that would be the last thing a manager would say to a player when he needed him on the pitch. I asked if there was a problem and he said, 'There is. We're five-nil down and it'll look a lot better if we only have ten men!' And, of course when I asked who had done the damage it was George Best who had had a blinder. I'll bet there was no manager who didn't know his name after that. For a young lad to be playing against Roy with such bravery and skill showed what a world-class player he was going to become. Perhaps Roy realised then that he was coming to the end of his career."

Well, even if Taylor suspected this, he was wise enough not to mention his theory to Roy.

❧   ❧   ❧

If his career was not quite at an end, Roy's time in the top division looked to be drawing to a close. A 1-0 win against Stoke after the 5-0 United debacle was followed by three successive defeats in which Bolton did not score and conceded nine goals. The Wanderers were in twenty-first place, four points adrift of Birmingham and looking down and out. Then something remarkable happened. The next six games netted four wins and two draws and suddenly Bolton were three points ahead of Birmingham with two matches to play. The turnaround had been so complete that the euphoria seemed to have gone to the players' heads, including Roy's in his role as the club's PFA rep. Taylor recalled: "We'd been discussing a special bonus for staying up and I was mindful to say to Roy, 'You'd better be careful, we haven't done it yet.'"

SURE TOUCH . . . Roy demonstrates skill and balance on the pitch.
(Bolton Evening News)

JUMP TO IT . . . Roy puts in some pre-season training with Eddie Hopkinson, Freddie Hill and Francis Lee. (MercuryPress.co.uk)

THE BOYS OF '66 . . . Roy in the role of Wanderers captain and elder statesman during his final year as a professional in 1966. (Bolton Evening News)

Taylor's caution was more than justified. As he explained: "Birmingham had Liverpool and Sheffield United to play and we had Tottenham and Wolves at home. We went to Tottenham, I had a good chance and then the keeper picked it up and kicked it down the field. It went straight to Jimmy Greaves and he stuck it in - 1-0. Birmingham beat Liverpool who'd won the league and must have tapered off. We lost to Wolves the following Friday night and they beat Sheffield United on the Saturday and stayed up. Blimey!"

Roy apologised on behalf of the team for letting the fans down and admitted that he could hardly believe what had happened. "If we had gone down at Easter," he said at the time, "before we started collecting points we would have been prepared for it. The position looked hopeless then but after the fight-back to within one point of success with two matches to play it is hard to accept the drop."

There was another setback for Roy as Bolton said goodbye to the First Division for fourteen years. On May 9th the scourge of left-wingers took his fighting spirit into the political arena as one of the Conservative candidates fighting for a seat on Bolton Town Council. He'd been approached by people he knew in the Halliwell ward to contest the seat.

Barbara explained: "I think it was because of his name that they wanted him to do it. We used to go to Halliwell Conservative Club and friends encouraged him to stand. He was pushed into it really – it wasn't that he was interested in politics." And initially the voters weren't too interested in Roy either as he came third in the poll. However a year later, in May 1965, Roy would top the voting to become a Tory councillor for Halliwell, a seat he held for three years.

Another matter that would help take Roy's mind off relegation was becoming a home owner for the first time. The property in question was a semi-detached dormer bungalow in Limefield Road, Smithills, about half a mile from where the family lived in Temple Road. "I can still remember exactly how much we paid for it," Barbara recalled. "Three thousand, five hundred and sixty-five pounds. My Dad lent us the £500 deposit for it and said, 'Don't tell your Mum, you've no need to pay me back.' He had no money, my Dad. I never did tell her."

Although Roy was now earning nearly £40 a week during the season, he still continued to work for a brewery in the summer. When he first became a professional, the money he earned as a labourer for Magees in Bolton and later Duttons in Blackburn was vital to supplement the reduced close season income but now there were a couple of added incentives. One was paying for the new home but, at the age of thirty-two, Roy was also looking towards the future. Duttons had recently been taken over by Whitbread, one of whose subsidiaries was the wine and spirits merchants, Stowells of Chelsea. Roy decided that the wine trade was where his long-term future lay and began lessons at night school to learn to become a rep.

10

WE'RE DOWN

In fifty-odd years of watching the Wanderers, my favourite seasons have been when the club has been a force in the second tier. I have a particular fondness for the three mid-Seventies campaigns, two of which ended in tears before a Frank Worthington goal at Ewood Park finally sent Ian Greaves' skilful and watchable team back up into Division One. My all-time favourite season is 1996-97 when memories of a grim first experience of the Premiership were blown away by Colin Todd's boys notching up 98 points and 100 goals. Bergsson, Blake, McGinlay, Thompson and Taggart! You gave everyone else's boys a hell of a beating! In a similar way the 1964-65 season, my first experience of the Second Division, is also one to hark back to with great fondness. There's something about being able to look at the top of the table with confidence, instead of at the bottom with foreboding, and that season with Davies and Lee on fire (twenty-five and twenty-four goals respectively), Freddie Hill (fifteen goals) pulling the strings and the only ever-present player Gordon Taylor chipping in with five goals, Bolton were in the hunt for promotion almost until the end of the season. They'd begun badly with one point from three games but thereafter it was more or less full steam ahead until the end of March when the steam ran out. Failure to beat promotion rivals Newcastle twice within three days in April condemned the Wanderers to third place behind the Magpies and Northampton Town. Nevertheless, it had been a season of memorable matches, none more so than in the Fifth Round of the FA Cup where a 57,000 Burnden crowd saw Bolton hold the champions

Liverpool until the 84th minute, when winger Ian Callaghan grabbed the winner with the first header he'd scored for Liverpool. Bill Shankly, who led his team to victory against Leeds United in the Cup Final three months later, paid tribute to the Wanderers players. Shanks, never one to dish out unnecessary praise to opponents, reckoned his lads would face no greater obstacle during their run to Wembley.

Roy, who the previous month had played his 400th league match for Bolton, was generous in defeat. As skipper he'd made a special trip to the Liverpool dressing room to wish the Reds well in their cup run and was realistic enough to admit that while he thought Bolton should have had a penalty when Liverpool left-back Gerry Byrne handled in the box, he wasn't exactly innocent either. "I've got no complaints," he said afterwards. "If we could have had a penalty when Gerry Byrne handled, they could have had one when I brought down Roger Hunt."

It was the first time I'd been in a crowd so big and I remember greeting the huge wave-like surges up and down the terracing with a mixture of exhilaration and trepidation. The fear was justified too, for when Callaghan scored, the crowd surge led to a section of the Great Lever End fencing not far from where I was collapsing, bringing back memories to some of the crowd of the 1946 Burnden Park disaster in which thirty-three people died on the Railway Embankment. Incredibly, however, this time only one person was injured as the barrier gave way and ground staff and police managed to shore up the broken section until the end of the game.

Bolton began the 1965-66 season with just two of the players who had lifted the FA Cup seven years before. Bryan Edwards had hung up his boots at the end of the previous campaign leaving just Roy and Eddie Hopkinson as the standard bearers for that golden generation.

However, only one of those remaining stalwarts would finish the season.

❧   ❧   ❧

Before writing Roy's playing obituary, a vital question must be addressed; how had he managed to miss just twenty games in ten seasons up to the start of his final campaign? He'd avoided serious injuries, of course, and kept himself fit by training hard. But you might expect that, given his robust style, he'd have fallen foul of referees many times and missed games through suspension.

In fact Roy Hartle was never sent off in his entire career. He was booked just once, and then not until he was thirty-two, for a tackle from behind. How had he managed this astonishing feat, given the number of left-wingers he'd sent careering down the grassy slope at Burnden? Even if we accept that referees in the Sixties were less inclined to pull out the notebook than they are today, it must be said that Roy was a lot cannier than many of the modern boneheaded players, most of whom might as well scribble their names in the ref's book before the match to save him the trouble later on.

Unlike them, Roy hardly ever got into disputes with the officials and his philosophy was simple. "If he blew his whistle, you walked away. You never turned round and had a go at him because it didn't do you any good. He's not going to change the decision because you're putting your hands up in the air. And I always apologised to him."

The phrase "hardly ever got into disputes" is significant because a report of the previous season's Liverpool cup tie describes how Roy "argued and jostled with referee Tommy Dawes after Bolton's frantic appeal for a penalty had been turned down."

And then there's the story related by Francis Lee about the time

Bolton played Aston Villa back when Wanderers were still in the First Division and, in Roy's opinion, their showman centre forward Derek Dougan was being his usual annoying self.

"I remember Dougan dancing around over the ball and doing a bit of fooling around," Lee said, "so Roy kicked him on the knee and he went down. The referee came running over and was going to book Roy so Roy said, *(Lee puts on posh accent)* 'Referee, do you agree with Dougan taking the piss out of me?' And the referee said, 'No, no'. So Roy said, 'Why are you going to book me then?' And the ref replied, 'Well, OK, but don't do it again.'"

Gordon Taylor offered the theory that Roy's compassion as well as his canniness saved him from bookings. "Even if he knocked the wingers over into the dip around the pitch he'd offer to get them out. For someone so strong and tough, he used to be so polite with the player he'd knocked over and he'd get on well with the ref. You wouldn't think he was part of such a fearsome defence. It was said that even the SAS would refuse to play them at five-a-side."

Sometimes, however, even Roy was shocked at what he'd done. While wingers were his enemies on the pitch at least, he looked up to one of them more than any other player in the game. So it was with particular shame he recalled kicking this legend in front of his home crowd. Roy explained: "I remember playing against Tom Finney and we clashed. Tom slid off the Deepdale pitch and he came back on, looked at me and shook his head. And I felt terrible because I'd done that to the great Tom Finney."

However, not every winger was a victim when facing Roy Hartle. As we've already seen, Derek Hogg became widely admired for giving as good as he got. And a young Manchester City player's encounter with Roy drew admiration from Fleet Street. In September 1961 the

Daily Mirror reported that eighteen-year-old David Wagstaffe played a fearless game against Roy in City's 2-1 win. The journalist was impressed with the youngster's bravery because Roy: "... is impressively large, slab-muscled, superbly fit and so completely ruthless that his undoubted skill is sometimes obscured. He tackles with the careering force of a runaway lorry. His philosophy could be summed up as 'I never squeal so why should they?'"

By the time Roy's final game against City came around in November 1965, Wagstaffe had been sold to Wolves the previous year and the opponent lining up against Roy was supposed to be Neil Young, who was not relishing the encounter quite as much as Wagstaffe had done. So new coach Malcolm Allison decided that the recently-signed twenty-three-year-old Mike Summerbee would switch wings from right to left and be the one to take on Roy. Summerbee recalled the encounter in the City programme before Bolton played the Blues in December 2006. He wrote: "I don't think I slept a wink that night or, if I did, I was having nightmares about lights flashing and an ambulance rushing me to the local hospital. But I survived the experience enough to hobble into the Players' Lounge where Mr Hartle kindly offered to buy me a pint. He was, and still is, an absolutely charming person OFF THE PITCH."

Which is where Summerbee spent a good deal of his time that day, according to future team-mate Francis Lee who was still playing for Bolton when the game took place. Remembering the encounter with a chuckle, Lee said: "Apparently Malcolm said to Mike, 'Just run the ball up to Hartle. He's so bloody slow you can knock it fifteen or twenty yards by him and you'll run him ragged.' So he knocked it twenty yards past Roy but he didn't expect the tackle to come in after the ball had gone. Roy kicked him waist-high straight down the dip on to the gravel. So that was a plan that went awry."

Summerbee also remembered the day with surprising degree of affection. He told me: "Neil Young didn't fancy playing on the left so Malcolm put me there and I ended up down the bank. Roy was one of the toughest men around - an exceptional talent. People were afraid of him. He was a tough opponent but when you came off he was a lovely man.

"In those days you had to be tough to play. Roy was a hard man but not dirty, just a tough, aggressive tackler. It would be very different for all of us today. The difference is vast."

Roy agrees. He said: "That was the way football was played. But we didn't cheat. I played against Nobby and Mike Summerbee and people like that and it was fair. He had a go and I had a go but there was no intention to hurt anyone. It was just hard football. And at the end of the day you were mates and you walked off together. And that's how it should be."

Nevertheless that City match will be remembered as a bad-tempered affair. It was part of a Wanderers revival after they'd picked up just one point in seven games during September and October. The only goal of the game of the game came after Lee beat two opponents before squaring the ball to left-half Dave Hatton who smashed it in.

Allison's switch of wingers may not have gone exactly to plan but sadly there was more than a grain of truth in the City coach's assessment of Roy's declining capabilities. The full-back was thirty-four and had undoubtedly lost some of his pace. Even so the end, when it came, was sudden and brutal.

Bolton had lost 3-1 to Preston at Burnden in a Wednesday evening game, with the Wanderers showing any number of defensive frailties. And two days later Roy was dropped for Saturday's match at

Birmingham, with Warwick Rimmer taking his place at right back and as captain. Syd Farrimond was also missing through injury yet Bolton's new full-back pairing of Rimmer and Charlie Cooper "functioned splendidly" according to Haydn Berry. Furthermore, in what can only be seen as barely-implied criticism of the old guard, Rimmer and Cooper "relied on close marking and constructive clearing rather than power play and reliance on the big kick."

Although Rimmer did give away a penalty, Birmingham could not convert it and Wanderers won the match with a goal from Lee. The following match, at home against Leyton Orient, Rimmer scored and was praised by Berry for his versatility, although he did admit Rimmer was more of a wing-half than a full-back. Meanwhile Roy was beginning his first significant run in the Reserves for ten years.

Ten days after the final match of the season, a 1-1 home draw with Norwich in which Rimmer scored, the club gave Roy a free transfer. Bill Ridding said: "It's always hard to lose players like this but that's football. It means we've lost two great club men in sixth months. (Edwards was the other). They were the greatest club men I've known in the whole of my career. It's a great loss to the club."

In the end it was a premature loss to professional football. Roy now accepts that, at nearly thirty-five, his First and Second Division days were at an end. What came as a shock and something he couldn't accept was that he did not seem to be wanted by any of the ninety-two league clubs.

So, after 498 full league and cup games and one substitute appearance, Roy was denied the privilege of becoming the fifth Wanderer to pass 500 games and join those other Bolton legends, Edwards, Lofthouse, Alex Finney and Ted Vizard. It was time to start a new and initially rather odd chapter in his life.

11

AMERICAN ADVENTURE

The call which began a strange new interlude for Roy and his family came in the early hours of the morning. When Roy came back upstairs to bed after answering the phone he told Barbara: "Some nut wants me to go to America." Barbara considered this surprising request for a moment and replied: "Let's do it."

It was March 1967, twelve months after Roy's final Bolton appearance and the 'nut' in question was former Manchester United player Freddie Goodwin who had been forced to confront a terrible situation. Goodwin, who played right half for United in the 1958 Cup Final, was new head coach of the New York Generals in the fledgling National Professional Soccer League in the USA. On March 1st, a few weeks before the season was due to kick off, Goodwin's assistant coach Alan Bushby, a close friend who had been with him at Scunthorpe United, died of a heart attack, aged just thirty-three. Bushby had arrived in the States a mere four days earlier and the tragedy initially shattered his friend Goodwin and then left him with the problem of finding a more or less instant replacement before the season began. So Goodwin contacted the PFA who put him on to one of its recently-retired members with a full coaching badge. That's why Roy Hartle received a night-time phone call and the offer of a two-year contract to work in the USA from someone he barely knew.

Roy had been playing part-time football for Buxton Town in the Cheshire League that season while working as a sales rep with Stowells

Wine Merchants. So in the cold light of day, he and Barbara were faced with having to reconsider their hasty decision to up sticks and leave for America. As it turned out, however, the firm was supportive.

Barbara explained: "When Roy told Stowells about the offer to go to the USA, they said, 'You must go, it's a real opportunity.'"

There were other considerations however, primarily to do with the children, eight-year-old Beverley and Russell, who was six. "But it wasn't as though they'd be sitting for their exams," said Barbara. "And it was always my ambition to go to America, I'd pen friends over there and I just thought it was a wonderful opportunity for us."

There was also a good reason for Goodwin's haste to appoint a successor. The National Professional Soccer League (NPSL) was keen to steal a march on rival new league, the United Soccer Association, a FIFA-recognised body due to kick off its season at the end of May. As a result, the 'outlaw' NPSL had its eyes on April 16th as a kick-off date. So within a fortnight of that call in early March, Roy flew out to the States on his own with Barbara and the kids set to join him within a month when they had rented out their house (which when they did was ironically to an American couple).

What sort of club had the new assistant coach joined? At first glance it looked an impressive set-up. The Generals, owned by media giant RKO, would play their games at Yankee Stadium, the home of the USA's premier baseball team The New York Yankees. After a few weeks, Roy was soon into the American way of things, bigging up the new league to a newspaper back home: "The set-up out here is tremendous," he told the Manchester Evening News, "and the money being pumped into the game is staggering. I must admit I was doubtful whether the game would catch on out here but now I'm sure it will." A bit premature perhaps, considering everything that's happened since but perfectly understandable from the standpoint of a new arrival keen to participate in an exciting adventure. But the follow-up was less considered. "Baseball obviously has a tremendous pull," said Roy, "but many Americans say it is a dying game and the (1966) World Cup really started a big interest in soccer. We are carrying that interest along." Now, while most Britons think of baseball as an inferior form of rounders, the game was then and still is woven into American folklore; almost a religion in fact. And its cathedral happened to be the very place where Roy's boys would ply their trade. While the Yankees, with a pantheon of stellar names like Babe Ruth, Joe Dimaggio and current hero Mickey Mantle, never had any trouble filling the 67,000-capacity stadium out in the Bronx, it would be a somewhat different story for the city's new soccer team.

Those early days, however, were still a time of hope and Roy appeared to revel in his new role. A letter home before he was joined by the family is full of excited news of arrangements made, air tickets booked, expenses collected and local children introduced to the mysteries of soccer. There was also a heartfelt appeal, "You asked me if there was anything I wanted out here. Please just bring yourself and the children – that's all I want in the world," followed by the excellent pay-off line, "You could also bring my tracksuit."

However, like the 1956 Bergen letter, the only other one from Roy to Barbara still in existence, this ends on a touching note. "Please take care, enjoy your trip," he writes. "It will be a wonderful experience for you all. Remember one thing. I love you more than anything else in the world and I always will."

Before the family arrived Roy had to get used to the new set-up. In the NPSL there were two leagues of five teams each, the Eastern and

Western Divisions, although teams from one would play those from the other. The points system encouraged attacking football, with six points for a win, three for the draw and one bonus point for each of the first three goals scored.

Some familiar faces were also playing in the league. Dennis Viollet, the former Manchester United centre forward, came out of retirement to become player coach with Baltimore Bays. In goal for the Toronto Falcons was Scotsman Bill Brown, who had played a vital part in Tottenham's double win in 1961. And turning out for Atlanta Chiefs was Northern Ireland international Peter McParland, who scored the goals that helped Aston Villa beat Manchester United in the 1957 FA Cup Final (and got away with a far more bruising challenge than Lofthouse's a year later when McParland's shoulder charge put United keeper Ray Wood out of the match).

Meanwhile the rival twelve-team United Soccer Association, which had actually planned to launch in 1968, had been forced into acting a year early after getting wind of the NPSL's plans. With no clubs of its own it decided to bring in sides from Europe, mostly England and Scotland. So the Los Angeles Wolves were actually Wolverhampton Wanderers, featuring Roy's old sparring partner Derek Dougan and Stoke City, with Gordon Banks in goal, masqueraded as Cleveland Stokers. There were also sides based around Sunderland, Hibernian, Aberdeen and Dundee United.

In total contrast Roy's clubmates at the New York Generals were from all over the place, the disparate bunch you might expect to pitch up at a new team in a country with no significant history of Association Football. They included half a dozen guys from the Caribbean, a smattering of Europeans, one chap who had been in defence for Scunthorpe United and a centre forward who'd played most of his games for Plymouth Argyle. Oh, and the bloke who would go on to win the World Cup for Argentina eleven years later.

Yes, Roy Hartle, putting his full FA coaching badge to good professional use for the first time, found himself imparting pearls of football wisdom to a tall, slim striker he knew only as Luis but who would become familiar to the sporting world as chain-smoking Cesar Luis Menotti, the man put in charge of Argentina in 1974 and who became the World Cup-winning coach four years later, confident enough before the tournament began to leave out of his squad a seventeen-year-old prodigy called Diego Maradona.

Freddie Goodwin explained how he had linked up with Menotti. "Through a contact we had in New York I was informed that Boca Juniors, one of the leading Argentinian teams, would be willing to loan us several players. I flew down to Buenos Aires to scout the players available and Cesar Menotti was one of them. He was a very experienced player who had a cannonball of a shot." In fact Menotti, known as El Flaco or "the slim one" was one of five players from Argentina who joined the Generals.

It would be great to report that, as Roy began to take training sessions, the South American striker would absorb valuable coaching lessons that would help secure him football's top prize a decade later. While this may well have been the case, Roy had no recollection of Menotti at all. Indeed he was absolutely shocked when, after researching into the New York Generals, I informed him that he had coached a World Cup winning manager. Shocked and quite proud. "Hey, that's something to talk about," he said, pleased as anything about the news.

Whether or not Roy's sessions made their mark on Menotti, they certainly impressed his immediate boss. "Roy quickly settled down into helping the Generals gel into a team," said Goodwin. "Many of the players came from different countries and spoke different languages. Roy did a very good job as trainer and assistant coach."

Those communication issues did cause significant problems, however, as Roy recalled: "It wasn't too bad in training because you'd got time to stop and point things out slowly," he said shortly after he returned to England.

"The boy from Haiti could speak Spanish as well as English so he could interpret for the Argentinians, and the Austrian boy could speak English as well as German so he could get through to the German lad. But once we started playing in a match there wasn't time for all that. It was impossible. The players were shouting for balls and getting nowhere."

Things would surely have improved if Roy could have stepped up from the dugout and on to the pitch. So that's what he did. After the Generals lost their first two games, Goodwin decided that the defence needed strengthening, particularly at right back. But where could he possibly find the kind of tough player he was looking for?

"He kept talking about me playing at full-back for the team," Roy explained. "And I said, 'There's only one way to find out and that's put me in and see how it goes. I'd like to think I could because of the standard I've been playing at for years.' He put me in the week after."

Goodwin could not have been more pleased. "Roy played most of the season," he said. "As a player Roy was a strong tackler and not afraid of using his strength. He would also offer advice to colleagues, which is important." Particularly so if all you can use is sign language.

Strangely the player-coach experiment came under threat due to an aspect of the new league's football in which Roy could reasonably have been expected to hold his own – on-pitch violence. This phenomenon had already been flagged up somewhat dramatically by Baltimore Bays goalkeeper Terry Adlington, late of Torquay, who told Brian Glanville, "You ought to see them. Animals, some of them, animals!" Roy agreed. "It's a very, very hard league. Very hard and very demanding." He was speaking from experience after a Toronto Falcons winger managed to get his retaliation in first. Roy remembered: "Just as I was about to tackle him, he jumped up and swung his elbow. It broke my nose and they carted me off to the hospital."

Barbara took up the story. "He came home and his nose was across his face. They'd set it wrong and he had to go to hospital in New York to have it re-broken. They only gave him a local anaesthetic too and it was hurting him so much because they were banging on his nose."

The broken nose was not the only problem facing the family. To all appearances they were living a dream life, with a nice big rented property in a town on Long Island bearing the very unlikely name of Hicksville. An old stone house on a thoroughfare called Jerusalem Avenue. The town was an ultra-modern place too, far ahead of the British way of life at that time. Barbara explained: "In those days they had the malls that we've got now. There were no little shops in the suburbs like we had here. It was a bit of a culture shock, seeing everything so big."

The apparent dream life impressed a Bolton Council colleague of Roy's who came to visit in June 1967. Councillor Donald Clarke, a director of the catering firm Percivals which owned Smithills Coaching House, was on a trip studying American business methods and on the New York leg he dropped in to Hicksville to see Roy. "He is enjoying the life very much indeed," reported Councillor Clarke, "and has settled down nicely with his family."

Councillor Clarke's impressions, however, were only accurate up to a point as little things had already begun to sour the Hartles' American experience. Cultural and communication problems for instance.

Barbara explained: "The kids over there laughed at Russell and Beverley for wearing sandals to school. They said Russell was wearing girls' shoes. He came home in tears because the other kids wore long pants and sneakers.

"Then a teacher got on to me and said, 'He doesn't know what a truck is. He keeps calling it a lorry.' And I said in England we do call them lorries. She had him in tears."

Another problem was the travelling. Not so much for Roy who accepted that when the Generals were playing in California, the six thousand mile round trip came with the territory. It was more of a headache for Barbara who, because they didn't live near any other footballers and their wives, was left alone for days on end in a strange country. "I got homesick when they played away," she said. "It was sometimes three thousand miles away and I was on my own a lot."

Roy put the matter in even clearer perspective by explaining: "I would sometimes be further away from Barbara than if she was in England."

The problem was partially solved when the Hartles moved in with some of Roy's playing colleagues who rented a large house on Long Island.

Barbara said: "It was good because we were all together and I could go out with the girls. There were about eight of us lived there and one of the footballers even looked after our kids while I went out."

The league was also facing problems, particularly its troubled link-up with television. It had all begun so promisingly too. The major channel CBS had signed a contract to show matches on Sunday afternoons. However, things began to unravel during the first game on

April 16th. Perhaps the station thought that in Danny Blanchflower, they had a pundit who would praise their fledgling project to high heaven. In fact, in his typically forthright style the former Spurs and Northern Ireland captain was merciless in his criticism of the opening match, Atlanta Chiefs against Baltimore Bays.

Things got even worse the following month when during a match between Pittsburgh Phantoms and Toronto Falcons, it seemed that every time there was a foul it was also time for an ad break. The match referee later admitted he had asked players to fake injuries so the commercials could be fitted in.

Roy's own rather comical experiences back this up. He remembered: "The referee said before one game, 'When you see me drop my handkerchief everybody stand still.' Can you imagine that? The referee drops his handkerchief and we all stand round for three or four minutes. And then you have to start running round again. That must have happened about six times. It was a farce!"

So, not really football as we know it and, although the points system rewarded attacking play, the football did not fill the stadiums. Roy said: "On a good day the crowd would be eight thousand, five thousand of whom had been given free tickets." In fact by the end of the season average crowds had dwindled to around three thousand. At least there were sixteen thousand at the first leg of the supposedly showpiece end-of-season play-off when Western Division champions Oakland Clippers beat Eastern Division winners Baltimore Bays 1-0 thanks to an away goal from Dennis Viollet. Six days later on September 9th 1967 the Clippers won their home leg 4-1, watched by just 9,037 fans. New York Generals finished the season third out of five teams in the Eastern Division.

Four months earlier Brian Glanville had wondered about the

viability of two leagues competing for a scarcity of spectators and concluded that amalgamation was inevitable. He went further with the assertion: "There is certainly no room for two leagues; it remains to be seen whether there is room for one." His instincts would prove spot-on. In December 1967 the NPSL merged with the United Soccer Association to form the North American Soccer League. The Atlanta Chiefs player-coach Phil Woosnam, who had cut his coaching teeth with Roy at Lilleshall in 1961 and recommended his old friend Freddie Goodwin to the New York Generals, later became Commissioner of the NASL. He oversaw American soccer's most celebrated era in the mid-Seventies when New York Cosmos attracted players of the quality of Pele, Franz Beckenbauer and Italian striker Giorgio Chinaglia. But even those famous names could not sustain long-term growth and the league finally folded in 1984.

The New York Generals managed to survive the merger of the two leagues unlike the Big Apple's other soccer team the New York Skyliners, of the United Soccer Association. But, at the end of the 1968 season in which they finished third in the NASL's Atlantic Division, the Generals too folded.

By then America was a distant memory to the Hartle family. Barbara and the kids had lasted six months in the States before heading home. Roy stayed on with the Generals until the end of the season and, after spending Christmas in Bolton had returned to prepare for the new NASL campaign in 1968. However, worried about the kids' education, he told the Generals that his family would not be returning to the USA. Shortly afterwards Roy too ended his association with the New York Generals and Beverley and Russell settled back into a more normal life at Colliers Row Primary School, where nobody called a lorry a truck.

Nevertheless in later years Barbara saw the whole American experience as a positive one. "It was good," she told me. "I'm glad we did everything we did." And, despite the taunts about his footwear, Russell regrets that they did not stay on for longer. "My Dad loved it," he said, "and I think a lot more doors might have opened for him if we could have stayed."

One door that did open when they got back revealed a possible career pathway to the Midlands. It came courtesy of a call from Tony Waddington, the Stoke City manager who in 1961 had lured Stanley Matthews back to his home town club from Blackpool at the age of forty-six and since then had specialised in bringing older players to The Potteries and revitalising their careers. Those who had had Indian Summers at the Victoria Ground included Jimmy McIlroy, Peter Dobing, Dennis Viollet and George Eastham. Now Waddington was offering Roy the job as his first team coach.

It was a tempting prospect as Stoke were now established as a First Division side after promotion in 1962-63. However family considerations were again a problem. "I didn't really want to go and live there," admitted Barbara. "I didn't want to be uprooted again. We'd been uprooted when we went to America and it was just after that. I've said to Roy since, 'Would you have gone if I'd have agreed to go' because I felt guilty. Years later I thought to myself, if we'd have gone Roy might have made a career in coaching."

Or management perhaps. Not long after qualifying for his full badge Roy had begun coaching at Breightmet United, at that time an excellent Bolton Combination side. And at least one of the players there thought Roy, with his placid demeanour, was management material. Ted Green told me: "Roy was a lovely quiet-spoken gentleman. That was the impression he made on me and my team-mates. He was also a calm and thoughtful coach and would come to watch us when Bolton weren't playing." Roy impressed Ted with his all-round personality too. "I played cricket for Bradshaw and Tonge," he said, "and Roy used to come down watching. He always remembered who you were and had a word."

Gordon Taylor is also surprised that Roy never ended up in the dug-out wearing a suede coat and a worried expression. Taylor said: "I thought Roy had all the attributes of a top manager and I was surprised he didn't develop more in that area. He was very calm, would always have time for you and treat you with respect. He was a real gentleman in the style of Matt Busby. I thought he was absolutely made for a managerial job."

Others did too - Roy's name was linked with the Rotherham job when Tommy Docherty left. And, closer to home, the name of Hartle was mentioned when it came to choosing a successor to Bill Ridding who stood down as Wanderers manager at the end of the 1967-68 season, after seventeen years in charge. In the end that job was taken by Nat Lofthouse, who later admitted that he should not have gone anywhere near it.

In his autobiography Nat revealed he would have made an ideal assistant but just didn't have the temperament to be a top boss lacking, as he did, the ruthlessness needed to make difficult decisions like dropping players. In many ways Roy was very similar. Although you might have encountered one or two arguments from the left-wingers union, Roy is too nice a man to be a ruthlessly successful club boss. Of course he was anything but soft and subsequently held down challenging management jobs outside football. But, looking at the really successful managers of that time it's clear that Roy lacked the cold-eyed pragmatism of Don Revie, Bill Shankly's obsessive drive and the couldn't-give-a-toss-what-you-think-of-me aloofness of Alf Ramsey.

Roy later formed the opinion that he wasn't management material and never really fancied it even after coaching in America. Barbara agreed, saying: "He said if he'd been a manager he'd be dead now because he worries too much. It's a stressful job when you're getting a lot of aggro from the fans. Nat told us he never should have done it."

Another reason Roy was not too bothered about getting back into football on the managing or coaching side was the fact that he had been given his job back at Stowells and his wage was already higher than anything he'd earned as a footballer. "For the first time I could go shopping and not worry about what we were spending," said Barbara.

Nevertheless Roy did not want to sever his links with the game entirely and began acting as a scout for various clubs including Portsmouth, Queens Park Rangers and Blackpool. And in November 1968 he was appointed chief scout at Bury, replacing Colin McDonald who had been offered a similar job at Bolton. He would share duties with Alf Walton who looked after the club's junior side while Roy was in charge of the professional scene. The appointment began a five-year association with Bury and regular trips all over the region to unearth new talent, frequently with his enthusiastic young son in tow. "I enjoyed it immensely," he said.

Russell remembered: "My Dad and I spent hours in the car together travelling to clubs in the North West. They were happy times."

Aged only six when Roy had finished playing professional football, Russell was "not old enough to appreciate my Dad's never-say-die attitude on the park" so the scouting trips were a new chance to bond over football. However a different kind of football encounter with Roy in his early teens taught Russell an awkward lesson that he has never forgotten. "My Dad was called the gentle giant and that's how I remember him at home," he explained. "He was loving and always fair with me but there was a line in the sand and I can remember stepping over it. I was big mates with the boy across the road and most Sundays, together with our Dads, we would play two on two. Halfway through I produced the F-word and I got my marching orders and an early bath. I did not swear again in my Dad's presence."

❧ ❧ ❧

During this time Roy did not lose touch with the Wanderers and was a frequent visitor to his old club. So he was delighted when, in early 1969, Bolton announced he was being granted a testimonial in recognition of his fourteen years service as a professional. Roy was only the fourth Burnden stalwart in the modern era to be granted that honour by the club following Harold Hassall (1957), Nat Lofthouse (1961) and George Taylor (1967). His testimonial committee set about organising the match for early March (a backlog of fixtures meant it was eventually switched to April 1st) and Roy contacted the stars he wanted to be there on the night. These included Sir Stanley Matthews who, at the age of fifty-four could still do a nifty turn down the right wing thirty-three years after first playing at Burnden. But it nearly didn't happen, as Barbara rather shame-facedly revealed.

"I got in trouble off Roy," she said. "He'd rung Stanley Matthews but he wasn't in. Then Stanley rang back while Roy was out and said it was about Roy's testimonial. And I said 'Oh I think he's got a full team. Can you ring back?'"

Even after a gap of over forty years, Roy was still incredulous about the incident. "She's only gone and turned Stan Matthews down," he said.

Barbara added: "When I told Roy he said, 'You don't say that to Sir Stanley Matthews.' I always promised I'd apologise if I ever met him again but I never did. But he rang back and he played." Barbara glanced up at the ceiling before adding: "Forgive me Stanley if you're listening."

So the great right-winger was pencilled in for the Roy Hartle XI with other stars including Harry Gregg, John and Mel Charles, Jimmy McIlroy, Roy Vernon and two of Roy's old Bolton team mates Harold Hassall and Ray Parry. Facing them would be an All-Stars XI whose members numbered Gordon Banks, Ronnie Clayton, Bryan Douglas, George Eastham, Wilf McGuiness, Malcolm Allison and Francis Lee, who had left Bolton for Manchester City eighteen months before in a £65,000 deal.

In the testimonial brochure footballers, journalists and well-wishers lined up to pay tribute to Roy's qualities. Bill Ridding was particularly effusive in his estimation that Roy "was well worth an England cap" adding: "He was one of the hardest tackling defenders I've ever known and had the ideal temperament for the game. He never questioned the decision of match officials, taking the rough with the smooth with a ready smile."

The chairman, Harry Tyldesley said it was "both a privilege and a pleasure to have known him."

There was also a tribute from Nobby Stiles who reckoned: "I've never heard any player harbour any grievance against Roy Hartle," before going on to tell the tale of one who might have had reason to. This was United winger Mark Pearson who, after getting on the wrong end of a Hartle tackle, was thrown back into the fray after touchline treatment only for the same thing to happen again. Nobby explained: "Mark was moaning after that through the match and then in the dressing room he was all smiles. In fact he was tickled to death by Hartle's comments after the second clash. 'What a case this bloke Hartle is,' said Mark. 'The second time I went down he quietly told me, 'If you're not fit, son, you shouldn't have come back on.'

"That may seem a harsh comment," continued Nobby, "but it underlines the kind of thorough approach a professional should have. So many people take no notice of an injured player and then he limps along and scores the winning goal. Roy showed he had no intention of throwing the match away by leaving an injured player unmarked." Or indeed un-marked.

Thanking everyone, including his testimonial committee, Roy commented on why he had stayed at the club after being dropped for the 1953 Cup Final. "The answer is simple," he wrote, "I was determined to show the club and public I was good enough and the only way to do that was to stay and prove it. I hope I did just that."

The match, in the tradition of these things, was a high-scoring affair and, said The Bolton Evening News, "a footballing treat for success-starved Bolton fans." Those 8,478 supporters saw the International XI come out top in a 10-9 thriller, with Lee scoring five and Eastham grabbing a hat-trick.

In the end Roy came away from the testimonial with around £800, not a huge windfall even in those days. So it was fortunate that his day job was going from strength to strength. He'd taken to selling wines which he described as "quite a sociable event." He was good at it too and it wasn't long before Stowells made him an area manager and later in the Seventies a director of the company.

By then the family were on the move away from Smithills. During his daily drive to Blackburn, where Stowells were based, Roy spotted a property for sale. Duck Hall, a cottage in Tockholes with a barn at the rear, was up for auction and the Hartles were determined to get it. But the deal went down to the wire as Barbara explained: "We'd never been to an auction before and they were all villagers who were there. We knew how far we were going. In the end there was just two of us and this man said, 'We'll be like this all night' so he dropped out. And if he'd have stayed in for another bid he'd have got it because we were dropping out then."

The property took a while to renovate and the completed work included the statue of a duck which Barbara gave pride of place on the outside wall of the house. It turned out she needn't have bothered. "Later I got a book on Tockholes and it had our house in," she explained, "and it was called Duck Hall because in the 1800s they used to work at home, weaving and duck is a fabric. There was Cotton Hall, Silk Hall and Duck Hall in the village."

The family was firmly established there by the time Roy and Barbara's silver wedding anniversary came around in March 1979. Realisation was dawning, however, that a move into the country with a teenage daughter and son had perhaps not been the best of ideas.

Barbara said: "Never take your children to live in the countryside when they're older because they don't adapt. They've got their lifestyle. We were like a taxi service coming picking them up from Bolton. Then Beverley got a car and she had a crash coming home late at night on the moors. Russell got a job at De Havilland in Horwich but never took it up because he didn't drive then.

"So it was the wrong thing to do really but then again it was interesting. And we got a fantastic profit when we sold it."

The new house was also one of the reasons that Roy called time on a promotion opportunity. Stowells had offered him a directorship at their base in Cheltenham. However, as the offer came in not long after the move to Tockholes, Roy decided not to uproot the family to Gloucestershire and instead began travelling down for part of the week. The routine became too punishing, however, and Roy asked for - and got - his old job as sales manager back.

Meanwhile Barbara had become a part-time receptionist with a scrap metal firm in Darwen, a job which lasted a couple of years – and attracted the attention of the police. "The books weren't right, apparently, and I was doing the book-keeping," she explained. "I did think it was funny at the time because the boss's wife always said to do this particular book in pencil. If I made a mistake and did it in pen, she'd erupt. They took him to court and they said I might have to go to court."

The family left Tockholes after just four years there and moved into a large detached house in Chapeltown Road, Bromley Cross. The move solved the problem of living in an isolated rural spot but also meant that Barbara's job had to go. So with Roy immersing himself in the drinks trade, Russell employed by another firm distributing wines and spirits to Blackburn off-licences and Beverley working as a nursery nurse, it was time for Barbara to begin a new life of her own, a top secret one which would end up in the national press!

The new departure was being a model – at the age of forty-eight. However, it wasn't the first time Barbara had thought about the catwalk as a career. Back when she was nineteen, she'd had the chance to take a modelling course at the Lucy Clayton agency. The drawback was the £20 cost, a small fortune in 1951.

She said: "My Dad offered to lend me the money but he said he wanted me to pay him back. And I wouldn't do it because I didn't think I could pay him back. Later he told me, 'You wouldn't have had to pay me back, it was just so you'd think I wasn't giving it to you.' So I never went when I was nineteen.

"Then, when I was forty-eight I decided I would do it in secret and not tell anyone, not even Roy. It was something I'd always wanted to do. The kids had left home and I just thought I'll see if I can do it. I was the oldest in the class. They were all teenagers and I was like the mother hen."

After a month at The Pamela Holt Agency in Manchester she was told she had passed with a B-Plus grade.

"I was so happy I cried," she said. "Roy thought I'd been in an accident so I showed him the certificate. Then I began to do photographic work, modelling clothes in a fashion house in Manchester for clients coming in to buy for the shops. That was good and it was full-time. You could also go on a shoot and get £50 for just one morning's work - and that's a long time ago. I enjoyed it but Roy didn't like me doing it.

"I did have clothes on – it wasn't a strip. I did fashion house work every winter but that was like a full-time job for a month every season. I did that for a few years. It was hard work; you'd be changing in a little cubicle with two other girls and trying to keep your hair nice. But it was an experience."

The story was picked up by the national media, including the Daily Express, Sunday People and The Weekly News. Predictably all the attention had a down side.

"I got some weird phone calls," said Barbara. "These creeps were saying can we photograph you. And Roy was getting mad."

Luckily for them, no "creeps" ever ventured within slide tackling distance of Bolton's former right back.

    ℮   ℮   ℮

Roy left Stowells in 1982 to take up a manager's job at Greenall's brewery in Warrington, a move he now feels he never should have made, for both professional reasons and due to the fact he was leaving at six-thirty every morning to beat the traffic on the M62 and arriving home after 6.30 in the evening. Another job, working for a wholesaler, was no more successful or enjoyable. However, it was a move to Spain in 1986 which eventually caused Roy and Barbara the most trouble.

It seemed like a logical idea and at first things went well. Roy and Barbara already owned a two-bedroom apartment in Marbella on the Costa del Sol, which they had bought four years before and used for holidays. The company which owned their complex had plans to expand and Roy was offered a job selling properties. Meanwhile Barbara had a good idea to keep herself occupied.

"I opened a shop there," she said, "I got the idea from a couple we knew there. I went in her house and she had all these cards over the table. She said she'd had to have these English cards sent to her by her family to send back again for Christmas and birthdays. So I thought what a good idea for a business."

Barbara came back to England and talked to Ron Wood, a card wholesaler who also had an apartment in Marbella. The upshot was that Barbara went back to Spain with £200 worth of cards which sold like hot cakes. Barbara wasted no time renting space above a hypermarket.

Then there was a problem. "Ron Wood came and measured the space for units and told me what cards I needed and shipped everything across," she said. "But they all got lost on the way and I got a call to say they were all in Barcelona. They promised me they'd ship them down to Malaga but they all went missing. So we couldn't open. Then they found them but I had to pay two thousand pounds for the units and cards to be transported south."

However, the shop eventually did open and was a great success. So much so that two-and-a-half years after it opened, Barbara received a tempting offer to sell. She explained: "We met a couple who had a business down in London. They wanted to buy it off us and they offered twenty thousand pounds. But I felt awful because shortly after we said we'd sell it, the boss of the hypermarket said he was selling up and wanted the space back. I was so embarrassed because this couple could have thought I was doing a moonlight flit but I assured them I wasn't. So it fell through."

Around this time there was a bit of good news as, after a protracted legal battle, Barbara got a portion of the two thousand pounds back from the firm who had shipped her stuff to northern instead of southern Spain. But by then other things had started to go wrong.

She explained: "We already had this apartment but, living there, we wanted a bigger one and they were building some more. So we said put the money from our apartment on to the new one and then we'd pay the difference. But it never got built and we never got our money off the first one because the company went bankrupt.

"We had already moved into another house because they wanted to sell ours to someone else. But we'd lived there rent-free in this bigger place for four years so we were luckier than some people who never even got a chance to live there."

"It was a terrible time," said Roy, who'd lost his job when the firm went bust. As a final indignity the electricity was cut off, even though they'd paid their bill, so they had to go to other apartments to shower and do the weekly wash.

"At that point we'd just had enough and wanted to come home," said Barbara. "But overall we'd really enjoyed our four-and-a-half years out there – we'd had different people coming out to visit us every two weeks and looking back we're glad we did it."

They were also relieved that they'd had the foresight to hang on to their house in Bolton, a cottage in Turton Road that they'd bought after selling their property in Bromley Cross. They had been out in Spain four-and-a-half years.

This low point in Roy's life mirrored the trough into which the Wanderers had sunk. After Bolton had slipped out of the First Division in 1980, the rest of the decade was an unmitigated disaster, the depths being plumbed in 1987 with a drop down into the Fourth Division. Fortunately the Whites immediately clawed their way out of the basement after one season due to a final-day 1-0 win at Wrexham, courtesy of a goal from the Robbie Savage who Bolton fans never booed.

But for the next four seasons, apart from a Wembley triumph in the Sherpa Van Trophy, the fans had little to cheer about. Bolton were marooned in the Third Division and even when we had a chance to escape, a 1-0 defeat by Tranmere in the 1991 play-offs condemned the club to another third-tier campaign, which would end in mid-table mediocrity. However, at this low point things were about to look up for both the Wanderers and for Roy. He would be coming home in more senses than one.

BACK IN THE USA... The New York Generals in 1967.
Roy is on the extreme right of the picture and future World Cup winning
manager Cesar Luis Menotti is second left on the front row.
Freddie Goodwin, the head coach, is extreme left.

POOL WINNERS . . . Roy and the family take a break in Massachusetts during the summer of 1967.

SHIPSHAPE . . . Barbara with Beverley and Russell by the Queen Mary in New York harbour.

SUNSHINE GIRL . . . Barbara does a spot of gardening at their villa in Marbella.

HOME SWEET HOME . . . Duck Hall, the cottage Roy and Barbara bought at auction in Tockholes, near Darwen.

MODEL PUPIL . . . Barbara after her successful course at the Pamela Holt Model Agency in Manchester. (PHA Agency)

BARBARA HARTLE

Height: 5'8"
Bust: 36"
Waist: 26"
Hips: 38"
Hair: Brunette
Eyes: Brown
Shoes: 6/6½
Specialities: Corsetry and Shows

THE PAMELA HOLT MODEL AGENCY
31 King Street West, Manchester M3 2PF
Telephone: 061-834 6741

12

BACK HOME

Even the great Nat Lofthouse had had his fair share of downs as well as ups in his long association with Bolton Wanderers. He'd clashed with the club over his tenancy of The Castle Hotel and, when his glory-filled playing days ended, Bolton's No 1 legend found himself mopping the floor and scrubbing out the toilets in the Burnden dressing room in his role as reserve team trainer. Promotion to manager had proved hardly more enjoyable and, after enduring two fretful years as team boss in the late 1960s, Nat professed himself 'relieved' when the club moved him upstairs into the post of general manager. He wasn't pleased, however, in June 1972 when Bolton sacked him from his job as chief scout. "This hurt," he confessed. "It came totally out of the blue and to this day I don't really know the background."

But, by his own admission, Nat could not keep away from the club that had been his life since 1939 and he spent six years in the stands and on the terraces watching Ian Greaves' team inch their way towards the First Division. Then, in 1978, came the call that transformed his later life. Bolton wanted him to run their new executive club.

"I didn't have to think twice," said Nat, who set about his role as executive club director with the enthusiasm he'd shown as a player. Along with Commercial Manager Alf Davies he made sure the club's vital Lifeline scheme had a constant flow of new members paying two pounds a week.

In the mid-1980s it was always comforting to see Nat on the

pitch doing the Lifeline draw in front of 4,000 fans waiting with less than bated breath for the second half of such classics as Wanderers v Hartlepool. It was also a reminder of how far the club had fallen.

Nat, who was made club president in 1986, was also responsible for looking after the 120 members of the executive club who met for a meal and drinks before the match. And by 1992 the set-up was so successful Nat needed another personality, preferably an ex-footballer, to help as match day host. So he turned to a former playing colleague.

Since he'd returned from Spain, Roy had been working in the office of an engineering firm in Union Road, Bolton, owned by a friend from Spain, self-made millionaire Eric Dutton. The work was agreeable and left Roy with weekends free to pursue leisure interests, golf prominent among them. What was missing from the agenda was football.

The Wanderers were hardly uppermost in his mind any more. He'd been out of the country for four-and-a-half years and even before that had not had much close contact with the club since his scouting duties ended in the early Seventies. However, when neighbour Nat called round with the offer to go back to Burnden Roy was intrigued. And it didn't take much persuasion. "I jumped at the chance like a shot," he said.

Someone else who joined the club's commercial operation around that time was Andrew Dean, now the Wanderers' Promotions Manager. He said: "On a match day Roy would come down and we got to know one another from then. If Nat wasn't available at Burnden Park to meet the sponsors, Roy would step in. He was very knowledgeable, could speak very eloquently and had nice stories to tell, not just of Bolton but players he'd played against."

As Roy grew into the job, this sociable aspect came more to the fore. Andrew remembered a particular trip to Arsenal. "We had to hold the coach up," he explained, "because Roy was still inside having a drink with the Arsenal hierarchy and the police wanted to move our coaches off. We were waiting for Roy who was still mixing and enjoying himself."

Nat himself had no doubts he'd made the right choice, describing Roy as "one of life's gentlemen". This, however, did not extend to his opinion of Roy on the pitch. He informed Michael Parkinson in a newspaper interview in February 1995: "I tell people that if Roy Hartle's mother had pulled a No 11 shirt on and run out at Burnden Park with the opposition, he would have kicked her to death."

This sense of fun and banter between the two former team-mates is also evident during the encounter with a well-known commentator in 1996. It came after the Wanderers' first season in the Premiership ended in relegation, confirmed by a 1-0 home defeat against Southampton and coincided with a visit to Burnden by John Motson. Motty, who, with Nat, had just finished talking to manager Colin Todd and chairman Gordon Hargreaves, takes up the story. "As I walked out a playful foot suddenly came out and tapped me on the ankle. 'It's a good job he didn't kick you properly,' said Nat. 'That's Roy Hartle.' "

Motty then re-hashes the old "unless tha wants gravel rash" quote, which he attributes to both Roy and Tommy Banks before adding: "I thought about asking Hartle to verify that quote but he looked sprightly enough to give me a demonstration so I made my excuses and left."

In fact it's extremely unlikely that the commentator would have had any cause to worry. Roy would surely have behaved like the perfect gentleman that he is - and helped Motty back to his feet at the earliest opportunity.

By this time Roy was once again a familiar figure around Burnden Park, walking with the aid of a silver-topped black cane, a legacy of two hip replacements due to arthritis. He was active behind the scenes as well, forming the ex-players' association with Eddie Hopkinson and becoming Honorary President of Bolton Wanderers Supporters Club. "Roy was a major factor in getting the former players association off the ground," said Andrew Dean.

❧   ❧   ❧

Roy's return to the Wanderers also coincided with an upturn in the club's fortunes. Under Bruce Rioch, the team was playing attractive football and winning matches. In 1993, Rioch steered Bolton back into the second tier - now Division One - for the first time in a decade. Two years later he took Bolton to the Coca Cola Cup Final and Roy paid a fulsome tribute to the manager and his assistant Colin Todd. "They have built a really good side and a first class squad," he said. "What impresses me most is that the opposition never knows where the goals are going to come from. Apart from the strikers (John McGinlay and Mixu Paatelainen) (Alan) Thompson, (David) Lee, (Jason) McAteer and (Richard) Sneekes all weigh in with the goals."

Bolton lost the final 2-1 to Liverpool but two months later they were back at Wembley in the Division One play-off final against Reading. And, at 2-0 down with a penalty awarded against them shortly before half-time, it looked all up for the Whites. However, Keith Branagan, who Roy reckons was Rioch's best and most important signing, saved the spot kick from Stuart Lovell and Bolton went on to win a truly thrilling match 4-3. "It was one of the greatest sporting comebacks I've ever witnessed," Roy told me. "I was so proud of the team."

Rioch left Bolton after the play-off cheering had barely died down to take on his short-lived role as Arsenal boss. The combination of Todd and Roy McFarland as joint Bolton managers never worked and a dismal first term in the Premiership ended in relegation with Todd in sole charge. However, that unpromising backdrop was the prelude to arguably our best season in my lifetime – and the final one at Burnden Park. A look at the record books shows that Bolton gained more points (98), scored more goals (100) and had more wins (28) than in any other season but even those impressive figures don't fully convey what an unexpected pleasure 1996-97 became. A largely settled line-up gave the side stability and balance from which flowed some of the best football seen at Burnden for years. A mixture of steel and skill in midfield was embodied by the tireless Per Frandsen and Thompson who, with Scott Sellars and Michael Johansen provided the ammunition for strikers McGinlay and Nathan Blake to plunder fifty-four goals between them. Even the final defeat at Burnden contains some retrospective consolation for fans as Chesterfield's three goals which knocked Bolton out of the FA Cup in the Fourth Round were scored by the impressive eighteen-year-old Kevin Davies, later to give a decade of whole-hearted service to the club. Bolton clinched promotion with five games to spare and said goodbye to Burnden in rousing style with a 4-1 win over Charlton in which, fittingly, McGinlay scored the final goal at the old ground.

Roy's feelings about leaving Burnden Park, the stadium in which he had first set foot as a seventeen-year-old nearly half a century before, were ambivalent. "I was heartbroken when they decided to sell Burnden," he said. "I'd even planned to have my ashes scattered at the Railway End." But he admitted that the facilities at the new Reebok Stadium in Horwich were "superb" and gave much more room and scope for pre-match entertainment.

Roy was so much a part of the club again that his views were sought on all sorts of matters. For instance he was in a unique position to recognise that the 2001 Play-off Final against Preston outstripped even his own greatest moment, the 1958 FA Cup Final in importance to the club, especially when money was taken into account. "It's probably the biggest game in the history of Bolton Wanderers in terms of finance," he said before the match at Cardiff's Millennium Stadium, which Bolton won comfortably 3-0.

The man who took Bolton to that play-off victory and back into the Premier League also came in for fulsome praise. Roy's fellow Midlander Sam Allardyce – born, like Dennis Stevens, in Dudley fifteen miles north of Catshill – took over from Todd in 1999 and had steered Bolton back into the top flight at the second attempt. In Sam, a Wanderers stalwart of the Seventies and early Eighties, Roy recognised a similar kind of determined defender to himself and paid him the ultimate compliment when he said: "The way he played he could have been with us in the team that won the Cup. We were 110 per cent non-stop totally committed players who always left opponents knowing they had been in a game."

Memories of that great day in 1958 were re-kindled the year after promotion when the club marked its 125th anniversary by inaugurating a Hall of Fame for the eleven players who had clocked up more than 450 games for the club. Joining Eddie Hopkinson, the holder of Bolton's all-time appearance record of 578 games on this roll of honour, were no fewer than four of his colleagues from the 1958 team, namely Bryan Edwards (518), Nat Lofthouse (503), Roy Hartle (499) and Doug Holden (463). The other six players honoured were 1920s stalwarts Alex Finney (530), Ted Vizard (512) and Joe Smith (492), plus stars from the Sixties and Seventies, Roy Greaves (575), Warwick Rimmer (528) and Paul Jones (506).

The ultimate accolade for Roy came two years later in August 2004 when the club renamed the Reebok's Emerson Suite in the West Stand, the Roy Hartle Suite. "That was one heck of an honour," admitted Roy, "I feel ever so humble about it but get a real buzz every time I go to the Stadium and see signs to the Roy Hartle Suite." Roy is in select company as there are only three parts of the ground named after players. (The Nat Lofthouse Stand and the Eddie Hopkinson Suite are the others).

The Hartle Suite, which seats around forty guests, doubles up as the players' lounge after the match. It is where Roy would entertain scouts from other clubs and the chairman's guests. Andrew Dean said: "Roy loved it because he got to meet a lot of former players who were now scouting."

And after the match Roy would hurry up to the Eddie Hopkinson Suite at the other end of the West Stand, where the former goalkeeping great was looking after the match sponsors. There, Roy would hand out draw prizes and mix with the guests.

The Roy Hartle Suite has memorabilia from Roy's career on display, including his 1958 Cup Final shirt and the shirt and shorts from when he was twelfth man for the 1953 Final. The items, including his Cup-winner's medal, had been due to go under the hammer in January 2004 but at the eleventh hour they were dramatically withdrawn from auction. At the time the identity of the buyer was a mystery and Roy said: "We were looking forward to the cut and thrust of the auction but I'm so pleased that somebody wanted the collection and wanted it all. It wasn't easy to decide to sell the medal but we decided it was the best thing to do. It was only being kept in a drawer in the house and being brought out now and again."

It soon turned out that the buyer was none other than Bolton

Wanderers who had purchased the lot. The entire collection, which also included a commemorative medal from Roy's only appearance for the Football League and even his old autograph book, containing signatures of some of the Busby Babes, fetched around £12,000.

Roy and Barbara used some of the money to help Russell establish his new life Down Under in Gold Coast, Queensland. He now runs a limousine service and helps ferry I'm A Celebrity, Get Me Out Of Here contestants around. I spoke to Russell when he had just arranged to collect Eric Bristow from the airport and was fully expecting to encounter a brash and arrogant ex-darts player. However, it turned out that that description could not have been further from the truth. "He was a true gentleman and I enjoyed his company," said Russell. "We talked about everything from football to the Queensland weather. I also had a great chat with Linda Robson off Birds of a Feather and she too was great to talk to."

Sadly the early years of the new millennium saw the passing of three 1958 legends. The first, Ray Parry, coached the Old Boltonians Football Club for a couple of seasons when I played for them in the Seventies and always remembered who I was whenever I visited his newsagent's shop in Newport Street. Ray, a delightful man, died in May 2003, aged sixty-seven. Eleven months later Roy's great pal and goalkeeper supreme Eddie Hopkinson passed away at the age of sixty-eight. The Hopkinson and Hartle families saw each other socially and had been on a couple of holidays together. In fact, not long before Eddie died, he and his wife Sheila had spent an enjoyable time in Scotland with Roy and Barbara. "Roy and Eddie could sit down and talk about football until the cows came home," said Barbara.

And just short of a year later, the stalwart centre-half John Higgins, another very close friend of the Hartles, died aged seventy-two. "We always kept in touch with Higgy and Thelma," said Barbara "and we visited them quite a few times in Buxton where they lived."

Along with Nat, Roy was now firmly established as a club figurehead and was honoured to represent the club at the opening of the new Wembley in May 2007. The occasion was the FA Cup Final between Chelsea and Manchester United and Roy was the Wanderers representative for teams who had won the trophy in the previous fifty years. To say Roy was proud to be chosen would be an understatement. "When the chairman rang me with the invitation I nearly fell off my chair," he told me. Phil Gartside, the chairman, confirmed: "I was delighted to put Roy's name forward to represent the club at the opening of the new Wembley. Nat wasn't very well at the time and it was a great opportunity for Roy to step out of Nat's shadow and become an ambassador for Bolton Wanderers." And Andrew Dean remembered: "It was a very proud moment. He came out on to the pitch and the smile on his face said it all. He's a very, very big part of this club."

Roy's presence at Wembley, his first visit since 1958, brought United no more luck than it had forty-nine years previously as they went down 1-0 to a Didier Drogba goal in extra time. It proved a much happier final for Bolton, however, as with United and Chelsea having already qualified for the following season's Champions League competition, the UEFA Cup entry for the FA Cup winners or runners-up went to the highest placed Premier League team who hadn't already qualified for Europe. This happened to be Bolton Wanderers and it paved the way for memorable UEFA Cup battles in Bolton, Munich and Madrid against some of Europe's top teams a few months later. However, by then Roy was fighting his own very different, and desperate, kind of battle.

LEGENDS . . . Roy and Nat at the opening of the Roy Hartle Suite in 2004. Roy's twelfth man shirt for the 1953 FA Cup Final is in the glass show case. (Bolton Evening News)

FORTY YEARS ON . . . The victorious Cup Final side in 1998 at an anniversary dinner in the Pack Horse Hotel, Bolton. From the left are: Higgins, Lofthouse, Edwards, Holden, Birch, Parry, Gubbins, Stevens, Hopkinson, Banks and Hartle.

13

THE BATTLER

There had been a warning of what was to come nine months before that Wembley honour. In June 2006 Roy and Barbara were dining out with friends at a restaurant in Edgworth, just north of Bolton, when he complained of feeling unwell.

Barbara said: "Suddenly I looked at him and said, 'Are you all right you've gone all red.' He said he didn't feel too good so the lads took him outside. Then when I took him home he was sweating and shouting at me because I was driving too fast. He was awful. Then he was sick. He went to the doctor's the day after."

What Roy had suffered was a transient ischaemic attack (TIA) or mini-stroke. Although the symptoms of a TIA are similar to a stroke – facial and arm weakness and speech problems – they are not as severe and do not last long. However, while not everyone who has a TIA goes on to have a stroke (and conversely not everyone who has a stroke will have had a TIA), it is a definite warning to take care.

Yet the message was nowhere near as clear-cut to Barbara. "I didn't take it as anything serious" she said. "They just said it was a warning. I didn't know that from then on you had to be careful. They might have made it clearer to Roy because he went to the doctors on his own. Roy doesn't ask questions like I do."

Nevertheless Roy began to have regular GP check-ups and one of the consequences was that he was told he could not drive because the TIA had affected his vision, another common symptom. But after a visit to an optician, Roy managed to get his licence returned, although

Barbara was never confident that he was altogether back to normal behind the wheel.

"I didn't think his driving was good but I didn't say anything," said Barbara. "He drove down to meet our relatives in the Midlands four days before it happened. It's a good drive and he was very impatient and bad-tempered. Which was unusual for him. But I never thought it might be a stroke coming on. You see at that time I didn't know that the other one was a warning. I've only found that out since his big stroke."

The meeting in the Midlands was with Roy's nephew Dennis, his wife Jill and relatives from Down Under. Dennis said: "My sister June came over from Australia in 2007. We met halfway at Trentham Gardens on the Wednesday. The following Monday, the day June went back to Oz, Roy had the stroke."

The same week, there had been an odd and unsettling occurrence for Roy and Barbara, who explained: "Roy didn't want to go to the restaurant in Edgworth again - and then we went the week before he had his stroke. That's ironic isn't it? He didn't want to go and I told him, 'Roy, that was a one-off'. But it happened."

It happened on the evening of Monday July 9th 2007 after a perfectly routine day. Barbara described the events. "He was in the garden and I was doing my cleaning. Then he came in and said did I want anything doing. I said no and he went shopping. He loved it. He'd bring home bargains that I could do without. He came home and said, 'I don't feel so good I'm going lying down'. That's not like Roy so I left him. I thought if he's having a sleep I won't go in. Then he got up, had some lunch and went to Moss Bank Park with our daughter and our step great grand-daughter. They were late coming home, it was about six o'clock. He said he wasn't very hungry but he ate his meal.

"I was sitting in the front room and Roy was outside smoking his pipe. He must have come in because I heard this bang and it was Roy falling down behind the kitchen door. I just thought he'd dropped something and then he shouted, 'Can you come and help me I can't get up'.

"It was very frightening," said Roy, "I didn't know what was happening."

Barbara added: "We went to hospital and sat there for seven hours with him on a trolley. Then they put him in this ward at two o'clock in the morning and I went home.

"When I went back at seven in the morning, it had taken hold of him. He looked normal when he went in hospital but the day after he looked like an old man. When he went in he had no other symptoms; he wasn't slurring his speech and his mouth wasn't drooping. He'd just fallen. The stroke hadn't happened properly.

"He just had a thing on his finger for your heartbeat. Not a doctor came to us all that time. Nobody asked him if he wanted a drink. There was just a cadet nurse. Every time he coughed she'd come to him and ask if he was all right."

"I blame myself now. I should have asked when is somebody coming looking at Roy? But they have skeleton staff at night. He kept wanting to get off the trolley and now I wished I'd said, 'Do you want to try and see if you can stand up?' But at the time you think they've got to keep still."

The stroke had affected the left side of Roy's body and left him unable to walk. During nearly five months in the Royal Bolton Hospital, he was first put into a general ward and, after pressure from Barbara, was moved into the stroke ward a fortnight later.

Barbara decided it was time that Roy came home when it became clear he was not eating properly. "He was so thin" she said. "Flesh was hanging off him. I thought it was the stroke but he wasn't eating properly. They'd put the food down and expect Roy, with a hand curled up and a tremor in the other one, to take his own pills and feed himself.

"But I didn't make a complaint because I thought I didn't know what they were like with him when I wasn't there.

"It said on the menu tick if you need assistance, which I did - he needed help. The way I found out was that Russell came over in October. We were in this lounge and they brought Roy's dinner in while we were there. Russell was saying cheerio to Roy and Roy couldn't wait to eat this food in front of him. I said 'Russell's going back to Australia, Roy.' I thought he'd be upset but he wasn't. I went to the window to wave to Russell and when I turned round Roy was throwing his food in. I said are you hungry and he said yes. That's when I realised they weren't feeding him properly. He could feed himself but not properly because he was spilling a lot. I used to get milk and yoghurts out of the fridge at the hospital to fill him up. I used to take things as well.

"I didn't talk to the doctor very often. I wasn't there when she came on her rounds in the morning. I only spoke to her once.

"So I asked if he could come home. They said I wouldn't manage. I said I'd get somebody in and I'll try. They tried to put me off but I was determined. I told them that I was sure he would have died if he stayed in hospital."

Roy came home in November and, true to her word, Barbara set about organising their radically changed lives.

"They were very good bringing the equipment, all ready for when Roy was coming home. The carers were coming in but it was hard getting used to it. He still can't move his arm but he can walk. That improved with having the physio."

In hospital Roy had been getting one-and-a-half hours physiotherapy a week, not enough in Barbara's opinion and when he came home, she was appalled to find that the NHS would only provide an hour of physio once a week for six weeks after Roy was discharged. Luckily the PFA stepped in and offered to provide funds towards having a physiotherapist visit their Astley Bridge home four times a week. The results were immediately apparent. In the months after he came home, Roy gradually became more mobile, and was able to walk short distances although still largely confined to the wheelchair.

Roy's old team-mate Gordon Taylor said: "We've been pleased to help him with a lot of the medical attention he required because he's deserved it as a great servant of the game and the PFA. It's sad to see him not in the best of health but it doesn't surprise me he's still surviving because he's a really strong character. He was the backbone of the club."

However, the stroke had taken a massive toll on this determined and active man and hopes of a full recovery were gradually scaled down. Roy's situation became all the more poignant when his condition was contrasted with that of his niece June Pawson's husband Ken in Australia, who had suffered a serious stroke in 2004 and was unconscious for four days.

Ken is the brother-in-law of Dennis Hartle, whose wife Jill said: "Ken was so ill that the hospital had asked his family about donating his organs. But he recovered really well. He came over and Roy met him and, of course, he thought he'd be like Ken. But it didn't happen like that."

Dennis added: "Ken was a bit younger than Roy and was fitter because over there they're always bike riding and walking. It's such a shame for Roy. But there again he's still with us."

Barbara was determined that Roy would not be housebound and took him on weekly visits to Jigsaw, a support organisation for stroke victims based in Little Lever. At first this was difficult for both of them; Roy because he was still coming to terms with his disability and Barbara because she was constantly on edge. She said: "I was living with a stroke victim and then I went out and couldn't relax because of all these other people in the same position. But we soon got used to it and made friends."

Understandably Roy was reluctant to go the Reebok Stadium in the months after his stroke but in March 2008, he relented and allowed Barbara to drive him to a match. The visit was not a success. "We had a meal," said Barbara, "and then Roy suddenly started being sick so violently that I had to get the ambulancemen off the pitch to come up to look at him. They tested him and said he had to go to hospital. So he finished up in hospital and we never saw the game."

The experiment was not repeated until early the following season but once their fortnightly visits to the match became re-established it was as though they'd never been away. "There are so many people who remember him playing," said Barbara. "Every time we go, someone comes up to us wanting to talk to Roy. It's really heart-warming."

With pride, Roy said: "When we go down to the ground now there's a man in reception who shakes my hand every time and he always recites the Bolton team from fifty years ago."

Barbara also remembers the time another man came up and shook Roy's hand. "He said to Roy, 'I wish you were playing this afternoon.' This is why he's more popular now because he's meeting people of his generation. They're still supporting Bolton but they say it's not like the good old days."

The numbers who remember Roy at his peak and want a word with him include those who work at the stadium. Dennis Hartle told me: "Not long ago we had a tour of the Reebok and the guide was overwhelmed when he realised he was showing Roy around. They'd got a conference on in the Roy Hartle Suite and the man said, 'I'm going to tell them I've got Roy Hartle with us and ask if we can go in.' We wheeled Roy all the way round the ground and saw everything. It was great."

As well as visiting the stadium every other Saturday during the football season, Roy also manages to get out and about regularly during the week. There are a couple of trips to the day centre in Thicketford House, Tonge Moor, for a game of dominoes, exercises, lunch and more chats about the old days. Once a week, Roy is taken into Bolton town centre by a member of the team from Crossroads, a charity which helps to care for disabled people at home. Age Concern also sends someone every Monday for a chat for a couple of hours. And then on Sundays, there's a regular visit to Harwood Methodist Church where the conversation is not always about the Almighty. "When we go to church everyone can't stop talking about football," said Roy. "I just hope he's not listening up there."

And throughout all this, Roy is still the same placid and charming man he ever was. "I think a lot of people in his position must lose their temper but Roy doesn't," said Barbara. "He doesn't moan and say he's fed up. And he's still got a good sense of humour. He's always joking with the carers who come to the house."

On January 15th 2011 Nat Lofthouse, the Lion of Vienna and kingpin of the 1958 FA Cup winning team, became the fifth member of that side to pass away. Nat's funeral eleven days later brought Bolton town centre to a standstill as thousands of Boltonians gathered to pay their tributes outside the Parish Church where the funeral service was held. The five hundred invited guests included a host of current and former players and managers as well as the remaining six members of the '58 team plus honorary Cup winner Ralph Gubbins.

Of Nat, Roy said: "The crowds at Nat's funeral showed just what the town thought of him. He was a great man and a great friend to me."

As well as the obvious sadness at having lost a good pal and long-time former colleague, Roy was upset that he could not step in to Nat's shoes at Bolton Wanderers. The club had indicated some years before that he would be President after Nat but by the time the Lion of Vienna passed away, Roy had had his stroke and fully accepted that the President needed to be someone who could easily attend club functions and carry out other duties.

As a Lofthouse post-script, I'm not the only Bolton fan who is upset that Nat was never knighted. Consider the situation. We have a man who scored thirty times for England, played his entire career for a founder member of the League, was named Footballer of the Year in the 1950s and became President of his club and a sporting icon in the Lancashire cotton town where he was born. Sounds familiar? It should do – as well as Nat, the description exactly matches that of the great Tom Finney who *was* knighted, in 1998. While not for one moment begrudging Sir Tom's royal sword across the shoulders, it's fair to ask why that other great one-club man of his era was not similarly honoured. Asked how he felt about this, Roy replied: "Tom Finney was the best opponent I ever played against and fully deserved his knighthood. But Nat was the best player I ever played with and it would have been nice for him to get one too. Why he was not knighted I'll never know."

ROY . . . at Trentham Gardens, Stoke, four days before he suffered his stroke in July, 2007. He is pictured with (from left) his nephew Dennis, Ken Pawson Dennis's brother-in-law, Barbara and June Pawson (Dennis's sister) and Ken's wife.

FIGHTING BACK . . . Barbara and Roy at a function a few months after his stroke.

In 2005 a vote from the fans produced a list of the Top Fifty Bolton Legends. As you'd expect it contains one or two oddities particular to the time it was published. For instance, who now would think of putting Henrik Pedersen (23) and Radhi Jaidi (25) above truly legendary names like John Byrom (26) and Peter Thompson (28)? And as for Florent Laville who creeps in at number fifty having played fifteen games for Bolton while Doug Holden and Dennis Stevens are nowhere to be seen ... well, enough said! Stevens, who sadly passed away in December 2012 after a long illness, was certainly one of the most skilful inside forwards Bolton have had and the same description could be applied to Holden's effective and watchable wing play.

That said, the Legends list is, in my opinion, a decent reflection of the players who have contributed most to Bolton's history and the affection and regard in which these names are still held, especially as five of the 1958 team do make it into the top fifty. Nat is, of course, indisputably in number one spot while, reflecting his record number of appearances, Eddie Hopkinson is at six. Down at thirteen comes Tommy Banks while Ray Parry clocks in at forty-four, probably a touch too low but there you are. And then there's Roy Hartle in eighteenth spot, a position which affords him great pride. "It's a fantastic honour," he said, "and great that a lot of younger people still think about the players from my era."

So that's Roy the legend but what of the legends that surround Roy Hartle? Well, they show little sign of diminishing. No lesser an authority than Bobby Charlton was still recycling the "chip him over to me" story - apparently Tommy Banks said it this time - before Bolton played at Old Trafford in January 2012. In the match programme, Sir Bobby also repeated Nobby Stiles' testimonial brochure tale about

Roy's advice to the prostrate Mark Pearson, although he compromised the story's credibility by having Roy speak like a baddy from the old TV comedy Brass, to wit: "If thee's not fit, son, thee should not have come back on to the field." Quite apart from the odd use of 'thee' instead of 'tha' it's difficult to imagine the well-spoken, cut glass accented Roy Hartle coming out with anything like that. However, Sir Bobby went on to pay the Wanderers of Roy's era a generous tribute. "They embodied everything you expect to face when you meet Bolton," he wrote, "tough players but a pleasure to play against."

Did anyone ever actually land first bounce on the gravel? Who cares? The point is that the legend is still potent, conjuring up the vision of a procession of wingers, flying horizontally like arrows from both sides of the Burnden pitch as Roy and Tommy got down to work. And it's often wingers themselves who come up with the tales. Francis Lee, who spent his time hurdling Hartle tackles during training with the Wanderers, remembers with relish the time Bolton played Everton when as well as (literally) upsetting one of their players, Roy managed to visibly infuriate a supporter. "Derek Temple, their winger was quite quick and I remember he went past Roy a couple of times and all of a sudden Roy gave him such a whack, sending him flying into the hoardings. And this great big docker with spiky hair jumped up and shouted, 'Hartle, you're nothing but a yard dog,'" added Franny with a delighted chuckle. Some Merseysiders held Roy in higher regard and another legend which you'll find on any trawl of the internet is that when Liverpool were playing Bolton, Everton fans would go along to cheer Roy as he handed out stick to their rivals. Liverpool supporters would repeat the process when Bolton played Everton.

Whatever the whole truth, Roy remembers his years as a player with extreme affection. "They were good days," he told me with a laugh, "but

I never hurt anybody." Roy's full-back partner Syd Farrimond, who now has Eddie Hopkinson's old role looking after match sponsors, agreed. He said: "I never knew of him injuring anybody. He was a gentleman off the pitch but so committed on it."

Andrew Dean, who as a boy would collect autographs from his heroes as they crossed the car park on the way to lunch at a Manchester Road café after training, remembers that Roy never refused any fan's request. "He's never let anyone down," said Andrew. "He's a very lovely man and I'm pleased to call him a friend. Roy is Bolton Wanderers through and through and a legend in the history of our club."

STAR TRIO . . . Roy with Bolton boxer Amir Khan and Bobby Charlton.

Not long after I met Roy and Barbara, I asked them whether their son Russell ever looked like following his Dad and making it as a professional. Both agreed that, while Russ was a talented player, part of the reason he didn't go further in the game was that he was not keen on taking Roy's advice, especially as a young player. "He thought he knew it all at that age," said Barbara.

Like a lot of kids, you'd suspect. However, if only to show that he has learned something from his famous father, it's only fitting that Russell should have the last word from ten thousand miles away. He told me: "I played amateur football for Turton for twelve years – a one-club man just like my Dad. I remember walking off at Eagley after a local derby and one guy said to me, 'Bloody hell, Hartle, you played well today but you will never be as good as your Dad!'

"I thought to myself that guy is stating the obvious. My Dad played five hundred games for Bolton while I am playing amateur football in a local league. I never set out to better what my Dad achieved and anyway I never had the dedication, discipline and desire that he had. I respect everything my Dad has achieved in professional football and feel immensely proud that I carry his surname."

THE END

BIBLIOGRAPHY

Roy Hartle's Testimonial Brochure, 1969.

Austerity Britain, David Kynaston, Bloomsbury, 2007.

Bolton Wanderers, The Complete Record, Simon Marland, The Derby Books Publishing Company, 2011.

Nat Lofthouse, *50 Years a Legend, as told to Andrew Collomosse*, Sportsprint Publishing, 1989.

Making Headlines, The History of Bolton Wanderers Football Club as Seen Through the Pages of The Bolton Evening News, published by Bolton Wanderers Football Club, 2004.

Wild About Football, His Own Story, Harry Gregg, The Soccer Book Club, 1961.

Harry's Game, Harry Gregg, Mainstream, 2002

Masters of Old Trafford, Peter Keeling, Robson Books, 2002.

I Am the Secret Footballer, Lifting the Lid on the Beautiful Game, Guardian Books, 2012.

Bogota Bandit – The Outlaw Life of Charlie Mitten, Manchester United's Penalty King, Richard Adamson, Mainstream, 2005.

Rebels for a Cause, The Alternative History of Arsenal Football Club, Jon Spurling, Mainstream, 2004.

Motty's Diary, A Year in the Life of a Commentator, John Motson, Virgin Books, 1996.

NOTES

Unless stated, all quoted passages come from conversations with the author.

1. Country Bumpkin

"I began to get worried ... called off" Roy Hartle's 1969 Testimonial Brochure (TB).

"I was a country bumpkin ... frightening one at that." Conversation with BBC Radio Manchester's Jimmy Wagg, 2002 (JW).

"... the view that these two years ... a category in its own right." © David Kynaston, 2007, Austerity Britain, Bloomsbury Publishing Plc, ISBN 9780747599234, p 372.

"I'd never met Tom before ... Banky who'd played in the First Division." JW.

"Tom has rather long arms ... when he looks like that." ibid.

"I played against ... absolutely unbelievable." ibid.

2. Making a Mark

"would be regarded as a moral victory ... high kicking." Austerity Britain, p214.

"Europe is now convinced ... of Soccer." Austerity Britain p 215.

"I had mixed feelings about it ... end of the game." Nat Lofthouse: 50 Years a Legend, As told to Andrew Collomosse, Sportsprint Publishing, 1989, ISBN 08597p33. (NL)

"I looked at one or two ... I've got a chance." JW.

3. Final Insult

"On Christmas Day ... sticks in your mind." JW.

"The only weakness ... like full composure." Bolton Evening News 2/3/53. (BEN).

"In three league games ... the soundest side on form." BEN 29/4/53.

"The so-called full-back problem ... unless injured." BEN 30/4/53.

"Matthews is a superb ... Blackpool into giants." The Times 4/5/53.

"had to concentrate ... emergency left-half." Daily Mirror 4/5/53. (DM)

"Matthews' performance ...architect of victory." BEN 4/5/53.

"We lost because ... into the ground." BEN 4/5/53.

4. 'Got Wed'

"I didn't think ... in Bolton." TB.
"the semi-detached urbanity ... or Bolton." Arthur Hopcraft in The Observer 28/4/68.

5. Gold Reserves

"That was the start ... absolutely incredible." JW.
"If someone wasn't ... cover for him." BEN 21/3/2001
"My point ... and big shot." TB.

6. Eleven Tenners

"has emerged from ... Midlands idols." BEN 6/3/58.
"A stirring match ... of this journey." Making Headlines, The History of Bolton Wanderers Football Club As Seen Though the Pages of The Bolton Evening News, Bolton Wanderers FC, 2004, p88. (MH)
"After the titanic effort ... on the Cup." BEN 21/3/2000.
"He wasn't everyone's ... out of both situations." MH, p89.
"If he hadn't died ... of them all." NL, p16.
"Mind you ... for league games." BEN 21/3/2000.
"We've got to win ... get that medal." Eddie Hopkinson in conversation with journalist Alf Ballard about Nat's retirement in December 1960.
"the black market ... to the stadium." MH, p90.
"A foul? Looking ... with referees." NL, p21.
"If I'd barged ... been sent off." BEN 2/3/98.
"I knew I had taken ... shoulder charge." Wild About Football: His Own Story, Harry Gregg, The Soccer Book Club, 1961.
"There are no bad feelings ... him enormously." Harry's Game, Harry Gregg, Mainstream, 2002. (ISBN 1840183667)
"It was won by ... York replay." MH, p90.
"What an insult ... for so little acclaim." DM, 5/3/58.
"Hartle also had an excellent game." MH, p90.
"Tommy and I ... we'd always regret it." BEN 29/3/95.
"Banks and Hartle ... their own Bolton careers." Giles Oakley writing on The Republik of Mancunia website.
"The first thing ... memory of my footballing days." Masters of Old Trafford,

Peter Keeling, Robson Books, 2002.

"We went in to ... was Bolton Wanderers." MH, p90.

"One of our party ... excluding tip." The Secret Footballer/The Guardian, 2012.

"Elsewhere on the route ... applauded the Bolton team." MH, p90.

"bringing the Rovers ... they would ever get." Bromsgrove Advertiser and Messenger, June 1958.

7. Back Story

"Not only did he ... 1958 World Cup." Daily Telegraph, 3/4/2008.

"I kid myself ... can't say I was one of those." JW

"it doesn't bear ... caps in the future." DM 4/11/58.

"It is his first ... player on the staff." BEN 4/11/58.

"Selection approved ... Middlesbrough centre-forward Brian Clough" Daily Express 4/11/58. (DE)

8. On The Buses

"Bolton have a defence ... are able to do." News Chronicle, 1/9/58.

"They showed ... of high quality." DE, 20/10/58.

"If Roy Hartle ... England full-backery." DE, 8/9/58.

"You didn't even get ... playing European games." BEN 15/9/2005.

"The team's star penalty taker ... temporary measure." BEN 1/9/60.

"My own came ... hard men of soccer." TB.

"Well done, Franny ... I knew it was time to go." NL, p45.

"You can't do that, you're not allowed to." Bogota Bandit: The Outlaw Life of Charlie Mitten: Manchester United's Penalty King, Richard Adamson, Mainstream, 2005. (ISBN 1845960650)

"You don't play for us you won't play for anybody." The Independent 14/1/2007.

"Our contract could ... That was wrong." Rebels for the Cause, The Alternative History of Arsenal Football Club, Jon Spurling, Mainstream, 2004. (ISBN 1840189002)

"There followed lengthy ... at present in operation." TB.

9. Football - But Not as We Know It

"Ipswich played it ... floodlight pylons." Daily Herald, 21/8/61.

"which helps get your hands stuck round the ball." DM 5/5/58.

"Over it all towered the figure of Hartle ... best shots of the game." The Observer

17/12/61.

"There was this lad ... if you can call it that." JW.

"If we had gone down at Easter ... hard to accept the drop." BEN 27/4/64.

10. We're Down

"I've got no complaints ... Roger Hunt." Daily Mail, 22/2/65.

"is impressively ... so why should they?" DM 18/9/61.

"It's always hard to lose ... great loss to the club." BEN 17/5/66.

11. American Adventure

"The set-up here is tremendous ... I'm sure it will." Manchester Evening News, 6/5/67. (MEN)

"The boy from Haiti ... and getting nowhere." The Observer, 28/4/68.

"You ought to see them .. animals!" Sunday Times, 11/6/67. (ST)

"It's a very, very ... demanding." The Observer, 28/4/68.

"He is enjoying the life ... with his family." BEN 8/6/67.

"The referee said ... It was a farce." JW.

"There is certainly no room ... for one." ST, 11/6/67.

"I've never heard any player ... an injured player unmarked." TB.

12. Back Home

"This hurt ... don't know the background." NL p56.

"I tell people ... kicked her to death." Daily Telegraph, 25/2/95.

"As I walked out ... made my excuses and left." From Motty's Diary: A Year in the Life of a Commentator by John Motson, published by Virgin Books, 1996. Reprinted by permission of the Random House Group Limited.

"What impresses me ... weigh in with the goals." MEN 28/3/95.

"It's probably the biggest game ... in terms of finance." BEN 22/5/2001.

"The way he played ... they had been in a game." MEN 4/6/2003.

"We were looking forward ... now and again." Bromsgrove Advertiser and Messenger, January 2004.

INDEX

Y

Lightning Source UK Ltd.
Milton Keynes UK
UKOW04f1457041213

222373UK00006B/334/P